THE JUDAIC FOUNDATIONS OF COGNITIVE-BEHAVIORAL THERAPY

THE JUDAIC FOUNDATIONS OF COGNITIVE-BEHAVIORAL THERAPY

Rabbinical and Talmudic Underpinnings
of CBT and REBT

RONALD W. PIES MD

Professor of Psychiatry and Lecturer on Bioethics and Humanities,
SUNY Upstate Medical University, Syracuse, N.Y.;
Clinical Professor of Psychiatry,
Tufts University School of Medicine, Boston, MA

iUniverse, Inc.
Bloomington

The Judaic Foundations of Cognitive-Behavioral Therapy
Rabbinical and Talmudic Underpinnings of CBT and REBT

iUniverse books may be ordered through booksellers or by contacting:

iUniverse
1663 Liberty Drive
Bloomington, IN 47403
www.iuniverse.com
1-800-Authors (1-800-288-4677)

Because of the dynamic nature of the Internet, any Web addresses or links contained in this book may have changed since publication and may no longer be valid. The views expressed in this work are solely those of the author and do not necessarily reflect the views of the publisher, and the publisher hereby disclaims any responsibility for them.

ISBN: 978-1-4502-7355-8 (sc)
ISBN: 978-1-4502-7356-5 (ebk)

Printed in the United States of America

iUniverse rev. date: 11/29/2010

The entire purpose of our existence is to overcome our negative habits.

- Rabbi Eliyahu, the Gaon of Vilna (1720-1797)

TABLE OF CONTENTS

ACKNOWLEDGMENTS

This book grew out of two convergent streams in my personal and professional experience. First, while I was still in my early teens, I was exposed to the ideas and theories of Dr. Albert Ellis (1913-2007), the psychologist who developed Rational Emotive Behavioral Therapy (REBT). I owe this early tutelage to my late mother, Frances Pies Oliver, ACSW, who was trained as a psychiatric social worker, and who used REBT in her own work with troubled youths. The second "stream" did not begin to flow until after my graduation from medical school, when I began a rather belated exploration of Judaic literature and philosophy. (Though I had been raised in a Jewish household, I had strenuously resisted my parents' attempts to bring me into the fold of traditional Judaism).

My love of the Talmud began, oddly enough, with a single teaching in *Pirke Avot*, usually translated as "The Ethics of the Sages"—the only tractate of the Talmud dealing solely with ethical matters. The teaching, as translated by Rabbi Judah Golden, admonishes the reader, "*Get thee a comrade.*" In Rabbi

Golden's commentary, we are further instructed, "If necessary, a man should *buy* a devoted friend for himself." (Golden, The Living Talmud, pp. 56-57, italics added). I found this notion of "buying" a friend so startling, it inspired a short story I entitled, "Hyman Gleeber Buys a Friend." The story focused on an old man who befriends a disturbed young medical student, and persists in befriending the youth even against the latter's protestations. I felt that somehow, the Talmudic teaching was tapping into some deep, subterranean current of human psychology—and I believe this still.

As I delved further into *Pirke Avot* and other rabbinical commentaries, I discovered that many ideas I had associated with REBT and Albert Ellis were anticipated or mirrored in the rabbinical literature. In particular, I found that Maimonides (Moshe ben Maimon, ca. 1138-1204 CE)—widely regarded as the greatest Jewish philosopher of the medieval period—had espoused a "rationalist" philosophy with extraordinary similarities to the principles of REBT and CBT. Similarly, I found that more "modern" rabbis and sages, such as Rabbi Schneur Zalman of Liady (1745-1812) and Rabbi Menachem Mendel Schneerson (1902-94) voiced beliefs with strong affinities to those of Albert Ellis, Aaron Beck MD, and other cognitive-behavioral therapists. Increasingly, I came to believe that rabbinical Judaism and CBT/REBT shared the fundamental idea that *by means of our intellectual faculties, we can understand, modulate, and "tame" our unruly emotions.* It is the task and burden of the present work to demonstrate how this idea is worked out in the history of rabbinical thought.

I want to acknowledge the great debt I owe to the late Dr. Albert Ellis, who, toward the end of his life, was kind enough to send me a number of encouraging letters in which he acknowledged the affinities between some rabbinical beliefs and those of REBT—even though Dr. Ellis could not endorse the theological belief system of the rabbis. Dr. Debbie Joffe Ellis was also instrumental in helping me understand her husband's way of approaching the therapeutic relationship, beyond the mere "bones" of REBT theory.

I am deeply grateful to the many rabbis and authors whose works I relied upon, including but not limited to Rabbi Arthur Green's astutely psychological work, *Tormented Master: A Life of Rabbi Nahman of Bratslav.* Rabbi Benzion Buchman was very supportive of my work and was kind enough to publish my essay, "Integrating the Rational and the Mystical," in the journal he edits, *Hakirah.* I have drawn extensively from this essay, and I thank Rabbi Buchman and Mr. Heshey Zelcer for permission to do so. I also wish to thank the editor of *Mental Health, Religion & Culture,* Prof. Kate M. Loewenthal, and the Taylor & Francis Group, for publishing my paper on rational-emotive behavioral therapy, which formed the foundation for chapter 1 of this book.

I particularly want to thank Rabbi Dr. Reuven P. Bulka for his time and generosity of spirit in looking over and commenting on my manuscript; however, I alone am responsible for any errors that may have crept into the text.

Linda Orlando and Ira Allen provided expert support and assistance in editing and preparing my manuscript. The staff and editors at iUniverse were also very helpful in moving the manuscript to final form. My wife, Nancy, was her usual patient and tolerant self as I labored for long hours over this book.

Finally, my mother, Frances Pies Oliver, provided me with the requisite "early exposure" to REBT, while my father, Jacob

Pies, instilled many fundamental Judaic values in me—even as I resisted embracing them in my youth.

Lexington, January 27, 2010

Addendum: All quotes from *Pirke Avot*, unless otherwise specified, are taken from Rabbi Reuven P. Bulka's translation in *Chapters of the Sages: A Psychological Commentary on Pirkey Avoth* (1993b). All Biblical quotations are from the Oxford Annotated Bible, unless otherwise specified. The author has made every effort to locate copyright holders and to obtain permission for use of material not in the public domain or within "fair use" parameters. He is happy to address any inadvertent omissions upon written notification to: Ronald Pies MD, Box 332, Bedford, MA 01730.

INTRODUCTION:
MAJOR THEMES AND INTERCONNECTIONS

J udaism has long been linked with the fields of psychology and psychiatry, but usually in the context of *psychoanalysis* and its practitioners. The most infamous example, of course, was the Nazis' scurrilous characterization of psychoanalysis as "the Jewish Science" (Frosh, 2003). In contrast, it is hard to find much written about the connections between Judaism and *cognitive-behavioral therapy* (CBT)—the form of treatment that arose from the pioneering work of Aaron Beck and Albert Ellis. (Ellis and Harper, in *A Guide to Rational Living*, do mention the Jewish philosopher, Baruch Spinoza, but only in passing). Ironically, CBT is, in some ways, more fundamentally "Jewish" than psychoanalysis, and the connecting veins that run between CBT and Judaism are extensive and deep. Indeed, the burden of this entire book is to defend and elucidate this claim.

But whereas the links between Judaism and psychoanalysis are not of direct concern to the present work, a brief digression on this topic may help illuminate Judaism's relationship with CBT. Specifically, the nexus between Judaism and psychoanalysis goes far deeper than the Nazi slur hurled at Freud and his followers. As Prof. Stephen Frosh (2003) has detailed in a seminal paper, "Psychoanalysis was also seen by many of its *practitioners*, including Freud himself, as having a special connection with Jewish culture, history, and identity—a connection which had made psychoanalysis 'Jewish' well before the Nazis made this an index of abuse… analysts and others alike could see that Jewish assumptions and ways of thinking were key elements of the psychoanalytic approach" (Frosh, 2003, p. 1329).

The complex relationship between Judaism and psychoanalysis is far too involved to review here; however, it is instructive, in passing, to note this statement from the *Talmud*:

> Rabbi Hisda said: A dream which is not interpreted is like a letter which is not read [it is of no consequence].— *Berachos 55b* (in ibn Chaviv, p. 53)

The comparison between a dream and a text reminds us that, at the level of the text itself, rabbinical exegesis has always distinguished between *p'shat* and *d'rash*—between, respectively, the *literal meaning* of the text and the "creative" or symbolic meaning that hides beneath the surface meaning (Katz & Schwartz, 1997, p. 28). Very roughly, *d'rash* can be likened to a "sub-text." This distinction has direct and obvious parallels with the psychoanalytic distinction between the *manifest* and *latent* content of a dream—all the ways in which, to rephrase the old joke, a cigar is *not* just a cigar.

But how does this distinction apply to CBT and its variants, such as Ellis's *Rational Emotive Behavioral Therapy* (REBT)? As we shall see, these forms of treatment emphasize the conscious, "here and now" aspect of the individual's thoughts—not the deep strata of supposed "unconscious" or "repressed" material so dear to psychoanalytic theory. Nevertheless, Ellis *does* recognize the role of the unconscious in shaping certain kinds of emotional responses. More precisely, Ellis distinguishes between what we might call *surface appearance* and *underlying structure*, in analyzing, respectively, the individual's *emotional reactions* and the *beliefs* that engender them. In this sense, CBT makes use of that quintessentially rabbinical distinction between *p'shat* and *d'rash*.

For example, in their classic text, *A Guide to Rational Living*, Ellis and Harper tell us that what *appears* to be a simple emotional outburst actually conceals a kind of "semi-logical, fixated, prejudiced, or bigoted *thought*" just beneath the surface of awareness (Ellis & Harper, 1961, p. 24, italics added). Such thoughts correspond roughly to what Freud would have called "unconscious" ideas. But for Ellis, the individual's irrational ideas are actually "internalized phrases and sentences" (p. 22) that are just below the level of consciousness. With some gentle but persistent probing, we can uncover the "deep structure" (to borrow Noam Chomsky's term) of the philosophy or world-view that shapes the individual's emotional reactions.

But aside from the *p'shat/d'rash* mode of analysis, there is an even more fundamental connection between Judaic philosophy and cognitive behavioral therapies: in essence, both assert that, *by means of our intellectual faculties, we can understand, modulate, and "tame" our unruly emotions.* We see this principle clearly articulated by the greatest Jewish philosopher of the medieval period, Moses ben Maimon (Maimonides, ca. 1138-1204 CE):

"The more mental training man has, the less affected he will be by luck or misfortune. He will not get excited over a very fortunate event and will not exaggerate its value. Likewise, if one meets disaster, he will not be disturbed and aggrieved, but will bear it valiantly." (Minkin, 1987, p. 389)

More than five centuries later, we find a similar principle articulated in the philosophy known as *Chabad*, developed by Rabbi Schneur Zalman of Liady (1745-1812). Although Chabad emphasizes the struggle between the "divine soul" (located in the brain) and the "animal soul," the principle of *intellectual mastery* is essentially the same as that seen in Maimonides. Thus, Rabbi Zalman writes:

"The evil nature states its opinion in the left part of the heart, which thence ascends to the brain for contemplation. Immediately it is challenged by the second judge, the divine soul in the brain extending into the right part of the heart, the abode of the good nature....[which then]... may gain the upper hand *and mastery over the folly of the fool[ish]* and evil nature." (from *Tanya*, chapter 13, cited in Mindel, p. 181, italics added)

Finally, both the rabbinical literature and that of CBT emphasize the crucial role of *individual freedom and responsibility*—in particular, our freedom and responsibility to "re-make" our emotional life, by means of rational reflection, practice and discipline. A corollary of this is that *we cannot escape responsibility for change* by blaming "fate," parents, or other influences from our past. A characteristic passage from Ellis and Harper states:

> "No matter what a person's past history may be...he only remains disturbed because he still believes some of the unrealistic and illogical thoughts which he originally imbibed. To become undisturbed, therefore, it is only necessary that he....energetically and consistently work at de-indoctrinating and re-indoctrinating himself." (Ellis & Harper, 1961, p. 51)

Compare the above with this passage from "the Rebbe," Rabbi Menachem Mendel Schneerson (1902-94):

> "Your first responsibility is to yourself, for you can hardly hope to civilize the world at large if your own life is out of sync. We are all responsible for our own conduct; you cannot blame anyone else for your decisions or actions. You cannot blame your parents or your teachers, your employers or your leaders. Nor can you blame G-d for making life so difficult. No matter how intimidating any obstacle may seem, G-d would not have placed it in your path without also providing you with the abilities to overcome it. Therefore, it is your responsibility to do so." (Jacobson, 1995. p. 154)

In the chapters that follow, we will explore these and other themes, moving in a roughly chronological fashion from Biblical and Talmudic Judaism to the early modern and modern periods. In so doing, we must not assume that modern cognitive-behavioral therapies—or therapists—partake of the *theology* or *metaphysics* propounded by these diverse Judaic scholars, rabbis, and philosophers. Ellis, for example, has usually taken a decidedly non-religious (if not atheistic) viewpoint in most of his writings. According to one unnamed writer at the Albert-Ellis-Friends.net website, "In relation to religion and God, Albert Ellis called himself a "probabilistic atheist," meaning that although we can have no certainty, we have an exceptionally high degree of probability that God doesn't exist." According to this same source:

> "In later years, [Ellis] wrote and spoke about similarities between REBT and aspects of Buddhism, with both philosophies teaching unconditional acceptance of life." (Albert-Ellis-Friends.net)

Indeed, in a paper published in 2000, Dr. Ellis acknowledged:

> "The constructive philosophies of REBT…are similar to those of many religionists in regard to unconditional self-acceptance, high frustration tolerance, unconditional acceptance of others, the desire rather than the need for achievement and approval, and other mental health goals." (Ellis, 2000)

Furthermore, in personal correspondence with me during his final years, Dr. Ellis expressed considerable interest in the connections between REBT and Judaic teachings, particularly those of Maimonides. Certainly, REBT's philosophy comports well with Maimonides' belief in "self-control," and with Rambam's more general "God-oriented philosophy" of self-control, as summarized by Ellis himself:

"God gave me some degree of free will and the ability to think for myself and control myself; and I can, with God's help, use this ability to discipline myself. God helps those who help themselves." (Ellis, 2000)

In any case, we need not assume that REBT and Judaic philosophy share the same underlying religious or metaphysical assumptions in order to see that—in practice—they have much in common. Both assert the primacy of the intellect in its struggle with the chaos of emotion; and, like existentialism, both insist that we must take responsibility for how we live our lives.

CHAPTER 1:
BASIC PRINCIPLES OF CBT AND JUDAISM

Among the wealth of ideas that connect Judaism and CBT, we can discern at least seven over-arching principles or themes:

- The imperative of self-awareness and self-examination
- The necessity of striving for self-mastery
- The primacy of behavior over "insight"
- The cultivation of self-sufficiency and equanimity
- The understanding and toleration of oneself and others
- The awareness that happiness and unhappiness are "internally caused"
- The emptiness of short-range hedonism and immediate gratification

Principle 1: The Imperative of Self-Awareness and Self-Examination

Corollary: Lack of self-deception

> "The Torah commands, "Do not deceive your fellow man (Leviticus 25:14,17). That is the actual *din* (law). What is *lifnim meshuras hadin* (going beyond the minimal requirements of the law)? That one should not deceive oneself."—the Rabbi of Kotzk, cited in Twerski, 1999, p. 94-95.

Self-awareness and self-examination in the Judaic tradition are predicated on the conviction that each of us must scrupulously and fairly assess our motives, actions, and characters. Both elements of this self-inventory—*scrupulousness* and *fairness*—are critical. We go astray, for example, when we either overestimate or underestimate some quality or fault.

Citing the Hasidic master, Bunam of Przysucha (1765-1827), Sherwin & Cohen discuss the first element, scrupulousness:

> "Self-deception is a common human inclination; integrity is its antidote…Just as one is proscribed from deceiving others in word or deed, one is enjoined not to deceive one's own self. In this regard, the Hasidic master, Bunam of Przysucha was asked: Who is a *hasid*, who is pious? He answered: One who goes above the requirements of the law. The questioner asked: What is the law? The rabbi replied: It is forbidden to deceive one's neighbor. And what is going above the letter of

the law? Not deceiving one's own self." (Sherwin & Cohen, 2001, p. 196)

Ellis's REBT also demands that we evaluate ourselves honestly and without self-deception. Contrary to a common misunderstanding, thinking "rationally" is quite different than "rationalizing." As Ellis and Harper point out, *rationalizing* in the psychological sense means:

> "To devise superficially rational or seemingly plausible explanations or excuses for one's acts, beliefs, or desires, usually without being aware that these are not one's real motives. Psychologically, therefore, rationalizing or excusing one's behavior is virtually the opposite of being rational about it." (Ellis & Harper, 1961, p. 67)

In contrast, REBT encourages—sometimes by means of pushing, "noodging," or cajoling the patient!—an unflinching and honest examination of one's true thoughts and beliefs. Psychiatrist Rabbi Abraham Twerski MD points to the traps that we can set for ourselves, through clever rationalizations:

> "People of greater intelligence are more likely to be more expert at rationalizations. Any psychotherapist will testify that the most sophisticated patients are apt to be the most difficult to treat, because they believe most strongly in their own lies." (Twerski, 1995, p. 112)

That said, for both REBT and the rabbinical tradition, our self-evaluation must be fair-minded and balanced—that is, *we must be fair to ourselves*. Rabbi Tuviah Basser, in his gloss on the Maharal of Prague's commentary on *Pirke Avot*, observes that the expression "knowing one's place" [Pirke Avot 6:6] means that one must:

> "Accurately assess [both] his accomplishments and his faults. If he does not evaluate himself accurately, but overestimates himself, he is in error…Conversely, if one can objectively recognize his personal faults, he will be able to recognize his shortcomings in his studies and rectify them." (Basser, 1997, p. 397)

In *A Guide to Rational Living*, Ellis and Harper offer strikingly similar advice:

> "Accept your own and others' wrongdoings objectively and unmoralistically: as misdeeds to learn from and to correct in the future. Fully acknowledge the fallibility of yourself and others and make due allowances for the possibility—indeed, the practical certainty—of your and their continuing to make numerous errors and mistakes." (Ellis & Harper, 1961, p. 186)

It is true, of course, that for Ellis, one does not attach moral *opprobrium* to wrongdoing, whereas moral judgments are intrinsic to rabbinical thinking. Nonetheless, both the Maharal and Ellis would advocate accurate and objective self-analysis, with the aim of *improving*, rather than condemning, oneself. Indeed, we see the cognitive-behavioral and rabbinical traditions brilliantly knit together in the comments of Rabbi Dr. Abraham Twerski. Commenting on the Rabbi of Kotzk's remarks regarding not deceiving oneself, Rabbi Twerski writes:

"We may think back about a sin we committed, or some inappropriate behavior, and we may severely chastise ourselves for it….Although this may appear to be adequate *teshuvah* [repentance], it is not yet sufficient, *unless we understand how it came about*, because only then will we be in a position to avoid a recurrence." (Twerski, 1999, p. 95)

Furthermore, for Twerski, we have an affirmative responsibility to avoid unwarranted self-loathing and low self-esteem. Rabbi Twerski writes:

"A person must know the truth about himself and recognize his strengths, talents, and worthiness. The great ethicist, Rabbi Leib Chasman said, 'One who denies one's strengths is not humble, but rather a fool,' and another prominent ethicist, Rabbi Yeruchem Levovitz, said, 'Woe unto a person who is not aware of his defects, and who does not know what he must correct. But much worse off is the person who does not know his strengths, [and therefore] who is unaware of the tools he must work with to advance himself spiritually." (Twerski, 1995, p. 166)

Similarly, Rabbi Twerski points out that self-deception can sometimes take the guise of humility:

"Feelings of shame and inferiority are universally destructive and they have nothing to do with humility… inasmuch as these negative feelings about oneself are not based on reality, they are false…[and] as we have seen, the Torah condemns falsehood in whatever shape it comes…A person must know the truth about himself and recognize his strengths, talents, and worthiness." (Twerski, 1995, pp. 165-66)

In short, for both CBT and the rabbinical tradition, honest and accurate self-understanding is the key to self-improvement. This means we must critically but fairly take inventory of our strengths and weaknesses, and resolve to do better.

Principle 2: The Necessity of Striving for Self-Mastery

Corollary 1: The intellect is capable of directing the emotional and physical faculties.
Corollary 2: Great effort and internal struggle are needed for self-mastery.
Corollary 3: The individual will never achieve complete self-mastery (anti-perfectionism).

The burden of the Jewish faith is not unlike the task of cognitive psychotherapy, even though the latter is not theologically-based. As Rabbi Hillel Goldberg succinctly puts it, in his book on Rabbi Israel Salanter (1810-1883), the Jew is called upon:

"To perform specific actions and to perfect his character…the Jew is called upon to undertake a twofold preparatory course of action. He must *develop his mind and must educate his emotions and deeds.*" (Goldberg, 1982, p. 144, italics added)

Indeed, *self-mastery* is a common theme throughout rabbinical Judaism. In the Talmud, we find the famous question of Ben Zoma (2nd century CE):

> "Who is mighty? One who conquers one's passions, as it is said: "One who is slow to anger is better than the mighty, and one who rules over one's spirit is better than one who conquers a city." (Pirke Avot 4:1)

Some sixteen centuries later, Rabbi Moshe Chaim Luzzatto (known as the "Ramchal," 1707-1747)—a forerunner of the Mussar movement—tells us:

> "If man follows earthly pursuits and is drawn away from his Creator, he is impaired and the rest of the world is impaired along with him. [But] if he becomes *master over himself* and unites himself with his Creator…he is elevated and the world is elevated along with him." (Twerski, 1995, p. 56)

Rabbi Twerski later addresses one of the issues that often provokes skepticism when some individuals are first exposed to REBT and other forms of CBT. Discussing Ramchal's admonition to serve God with joy, Twerski asks:

> "How…can there be a commandment, 'You shall rejoice' (Deuteronomy 16:15), as if there were a button one could push to turn on *simchah* [joy]? Perhaps there is no button to push, but we are capable of having far greater mastery of our emotions than we think… *Affect is largely dependent on cognition.* We are happy

when we win a huge prize because our cognition is that having money is good…if we rethink our values, then our cognition, our ideas of what is good, may change, and along with that our affects can change." (Twerski, 1995, p. 255-56, italics added)

One could not hope for a more succinct statement of the chief principles underlying CBT!

Maimonides went far beyond the limited claim that our cognitions determine our feelings. He went so far as to say that *our very organs* are radically influenced, if not controlled, by our thoughts—essentially a presentiment of modern psychosomatic medicine. As Maimonides puts it in his *Guide for the Perplexed* (Part I, chap LXXII):

> …Man has been endowed with intellectual faculties which enable him to think, consider and act…and to *control every organ of his body*, causing both the principal and secondary organs to perform their respective functions." (Maimonides, 1956, p. 118, italics added)

In the same section of his *Guide*, Maimonides writes that "The intellect is the highest of all faculties of living creatures." Similarly, the Maharal (Rabbi Yehuda Loew of Prague, 1512-1609), discussing *Pirkei Avot* 4:1, writes, "The measure of human strength is self-discipline, which is the power of the intellect to direct the physical faculties according to what is right or wrong" (Basser, 1997, p. 214).

Self-discipline does not come easy, of course. Thus, Ellis and Harper note, "The greater your loss or frustration is in life, the more philosophic you must force yourself to become in regard to it" (Ellis & Harper, 1961, p. 118). They go on to say:

> "It is very difficult for the average or even the above-average individual to keep fighting against his or her normal tendencies to give up easily on hard tasks, to put off till tomorrow what really should be done today and to slacken self-discipline long before it automatically develops its own momentum and begins to maintain itself with relatively little effort. All right, so it's hard. But it still continually has to be done." (Ellis and Harper, 1961, p. 149)

The rabbis, too, understood that self-mastery does not come easily, and it is never a task we complete in this life. Thus, as Ramchal reminds us, "Man was not created for tranquility, but to struggle and toil…as is written in Job (5:7), 'Man is born to labor.' If one accepts this, he will find the Divine service" (Twerski, 1995, p. 123). Yet the Divine service can be frustrating and demanding. As Rabbi Raymond Beyda has observed:

> "In order to grow and reach new heights *Hashem* [the Lord] confronts the human being with obstacles and tests. He does not do it to find out what you are going to do in the test situation—He already knows that. The test is an opportunity to grow from the situation—and even failure presents a positive side. If you analyze your defeat you can usually discover a positive learning experience." (Beyda, 2004)

In sum, from both the cognitive-behavioral and rabbinical perspectives, the intellect is capable of directing the emotional faculties so as to change the way we feel about whatever may befall us. However, great effort on a sustained basis is required to maintain our emotional equilibrium, and none of us will achieve complete mastery over the emotions. Nevertheless, we must not cease our efforts, or allow a pointless quest for perfection to deter us from acting with the personal resources we have available. As Rabbi Tarfon reminds us (*Pirke Avot* 2:21), "It is not your duty to complete the work, but neither are you free to desist from it."

Finally, as Rabbi Beyda observes, even our failings can open us up to new possibilities for growth. A modern Jewish sage—the singer and songwriter, Leonard Cohen—expresses a similar idea in these lyrics from his song, *Anthem*:

> *Ring the bells that still can ring,*
> *Forget your perfect offering.*
> *There is a crack in everything—*
> *That's how the light gets in.*

Principle 3: The Primacy of Behavior over "Insight"

Corollary: Self-destructive habits must be overcome.
Corollary: Partial effort counts.

When the late Dr. Albert Ellis first developed his treatment, he called it "Rational Emotive Therapy" (RET). In later years, he changed the name to REBT—Rational Emotive *Behavioral* Therapy. This modification was in recognition of the crucial role not merely of "thinking rationally," but of practicing rational and constructive *behaviors*. It was also Ellis's great insight to argue—counter-intuitively, and contrary to many other theoretical models—that changing one's *behavior* could actually modify one's *feelings*. A number of experimental studies in cognitive psychology have since confirmed this view. As Ellis and Harper (1961) put it:

> "Don't just think: *act*! Years or decades of past fright and inertia may almost always be overcome by days or weeks of present forced practice...thinking and doing; these are the unmagical keys that will unlock almost any chest of past defeats and turn them into possible present and future victories." (Ellis and Harper, 1961, p. 162)

Consonant with REBT, the Judaic tradition generally emphasizes how the pious individual should *act*, not how he or she should *feel*. Thus, as Rabbi Bradley S. Artson observes (Artson, 2001, p. 127), the Torah does not insist that we *love* our parents; rather, we are commanded by the *mitzvah* of *kibbud av va-em* to *honor* our parents [*kibbud*=honor]. As Artson puts it:

> "Given the profound complexity of our emotions toward our parents, it would be impossible to mandate our feelings toward them. But our *behavior* is another matter." (Artson, 2001, p. 127)

In the rabbinical tradition as well, *practice* is also paramount. The Talmud tells us, "Not learning, but *doing*" (Pirkei 1:17). Similarly, the Talmud teaches that *behavior itself* may actually transform one's initial *motive* for the behavior. Thus:

"Rav Yehuda said in the name of Rav: "A person should always occupy himself with Torah and mitzvoth, even if he does it for ulterior motives, because from doing it for selfish reasons, eventually he will come to do it for the sake of Heaven." (*Sotah 47a*; in ibn Chaviv, 1999, p. 478)

Furthermore, the Talmud teaches us that good behavior begets good behavior; i.e., "one mitzvah leads to another mitzvah" (Pirke Avot 4:2). On this point, Rabbi Raphael Pelcovitz comments as follows:

"Every act creates a habit, and man becomes adept at doing what he practices all the time. Hence, a mitzvah does not exist in a vacuum…but rather, brings other mittzvos in its wake. This is the greatest reward, not in the sense of payment, but in creating and developing man's character." (Sforno, 1996, pp. 104-05)

The rabbinical tradition is not alone in this view, of course. In the Hindu tradition, we find, in the ancient text of the *Upanishads*, the statement, "According as one acts, according as one conducts himself, so does he become. The doer of good becomes good. The doer of evil becomes evil" (Severy, 1971, p. 163).

Nearly a millennia after the Talmud was redacted, Rabbi Moshe ben Nachman (1194-1270)—known as Ramban—propounded a behaviorally-based method of altering one's character that presciently anticipated modern CBT. In a letter to his son, for example, Ramban explains how achieving humility first requires control of one's anger. And how is anger to be controlled? Ramban writes:

"Get into the habit of always speaking calmly to everyone. This will prevent you from anger… [then]… Once you have distanced yourself from anger, the quality of humility will enter your heart." [*Iggeres HaRamban*]

In short, if you habitually *speak* as if you are not angry, you will avoid actually *being* angry. Ramban then goes on to describe a certain manner of walking and conducting oneself that is conducive to humility, such as walking "with your head bowed, your eyes looking down to the ground and your heart focusing on Hashem." As Rabbi Dr. Abraham Twerski observes, "If one adopts these behaviors, it is likely that they will impact on him so that he indeed begins to *feel* humble" (Twerski, 1999, p. 207). Moreover, Dr. Twerski notes, "Recently, behavioral schools of psychology have come to the fore, whose emphasis is primarily on changing the pathologic behavior, leaving insight to a later date" (p. 206).

The primacy of behavior over mere thought is also brought out in the writing of Rabbi Israel Salanter (1810-83), the founder of the *Mussar* movement, who emphasizes the importance of *repetition and practice*:

"Impassioned speech and thought will not affect behavior unless employed habitually—for years— whereupon the impressions left after countless instances '…implant themselves as an immovable stake, a lasting nature'." (Goldberg, 1982, p. 140)

Goldberg elaborates on Rabbi Israel's views, as follows:

"Rabbi Israel describes a method of transmuting both the inner self and external behavior, which amounts to habit. He writes that the more one observes commandments precisely as they are defined in *halakha* [law], the more one weakens one's inclinations that run counter" to moral action. (Goldberg, 1982, p. 141)

Indeed, for Rabbi Salanter—as for cognitive-behavioral therapists—reason alone cannot alter our inclination to engage in self-destructive or injurious behavior ("urges to sin"). Rather, "it is necessary to engage in *habitual self-restraint*" (Goldberg, 1982, p. 143, italics added).

Cognitive-behavioral therapists apply these concepts not only to negative emotions, such as anger, but also to positive ones. For example, Twerski notes, "External behavior *can* influence one's internal feelings. Acting *as if* one were happy may actually mitigate one's dejection" (Twerski, 1999, p. 60).

Principle 4: Cultivating Self-Sufficiency and Equanimity

Corollary: Reducing "neediness" by recognizing what is truly necessary
Corollary: Accepting discomfort, loss, and suffering

Self-sufficiency is an important character trait in Judaism. But we must immediately qualify this claim by noting that, by self-sufficiency, the rabbis do not have in mind a state of haughty isolation, or disgruntled indifference to the larger needs of the community. On the contrary, Rabbi Hillel (ca. 110 BCE-10 CE) admonishes us, "Do not separate yourself from the community" (Pirke Avot 2:5). Rather, by self-sufficiency, the rabbis had in mind something resembling what psychologists might call, "healthy autonomy," and what the ancient Stoics called *ataraxia*—very roughly, *"serenity"* or *"freedom from troubles."* A related term from the Stoics is *euroia*, which may be translated as "equanimity" (Seddon, 2005, pp.111, 144). Tightly linked with self-sufficiency are two related faculties: (1) an understanding of what one *truly needs* in order to be fulfilled, happy, and productive in life; and (2) the ability to accept and tolerate discomfort, loss, and suffering.

Thus, for the Maharal (Rabbi Yehuda Loew of Prague, ca. 1520-1609), the trait known as "acceptance of suffering" (Pirke Avot 6:6) means "reducing the constant neediness that accompanies dependence on the material things of life" (Basser, 1997, p. 395). Indeed, aside from food, water, oxygen, shelter, and freedom from severe bodily harm, our genuine "needs" in life are very few. This idea is absolutely central to Albert Ellis's philosophy and practice. Thus, Ellis and Harper write:

> "So you are deprived! Will your wailing and moaning bring back your loved one? Will your ranting at fate really make you feel better? Why not, instead, maturely accept the inevitable, however unpleasant it may be?" (Ellis & Harper, 1961, p. 113)

And similarly:

> "No matter what happens to you, with the exception of prolonged, intractable, physical pain, we do not think it necessary for you to remain unhappy for more than a very short while." (Ellis & Harper, 1961, p. 70)

The Judaic tradition stresses the importance of self-sufficiency on a number of levels. On the most concrete and mundane level, the individual must be *economically* self-sufficient. Thus, the Maharal writes:

> "Although it is improper for a person to be avid in pursuing wealth, it is…[appropriate] that he make provision not to be dependent on people, because this is a defect in a person… It is for this reason that our sages said (Pesahim 113a): 'Be a stripper of the carcasses of dead animals in the street, but do not be dependent on people'." (from *Netivot Olam, Asher 2*, cited in Bokser, 1981, p. 160)

But the rabbinical concept of self-sufficiency goes beyond mere economic independence. For the rabbis, self-sufficiency is what we nowadays might call "a state of mind;" or, more precisely, a *quality of one's thought and character*. As Rabbi Tuvia Basser observes, in his discussion of *Pirke Avot* 4:1:

> "Ben Zoma describes the rich person whose wealth is not in the bank, but in his personality…he feels that he lacks nothing; he appreciates what he has; and he enjoys the tranquility that comes from feeling secure and independent." (Basser, 1997, p. 215)

Maimonides, too, in his *Hygiene of the Soul*, distinguishes between necessary and unnecessary (if not frivolous) concerns, and links this distinction with personal happiness. Through consideration of ethical and philosophical principles:

"The mind becomes strong *and regards the important as important and the unimportant as unimportant.* Thus, affects become lessened, bad thoughts disappear, fear is taken away, and the mind is cheerful, as well as the whole person." (Savitz, 1932, p. 83, italics added)

Similarly, in his *Guide for the Perplexed* (Part III, Chapter XII), Maimonides argues:

"Those who are ignorant and perverse in their thought are constantly in trouble and pain because they cannot get as much of the superfluous things as a certain other person possesses...all the difficulties and troubles we meet in this respect are due to the desire for superfluous things; when we seek unnecessary things, we have difficulty even in finding that which is indispensable." (Maimonides, 1956, pp. 270-271)

Ellis and Harper speak forcefully to our potential for self-sufficiency, if only we discipline our mind and spirit:

"Accidents and physical ailments do occur. Environmental circumstances sometimes are impossibly constricting. War and famine, pestilence and destruction still...show their ugly fangs. But the human spirit, when freed of ignorance and cant, has remarkable resiliency. However bowed and bent it may temporarily be, it still may throw off its unthinking... chains, and rise above...[its misfortunes]." (Ellis and Harper, 1961, p. 188)

Principle 5: Understanding and Tolerating the Behavior of Oneself and Others

Corollary: Never confuse an individual with his acts, or a person who acts badly with a bad person.

Corollary: We can correct our self-defeating behaviors without indulging in self-punishment or self-abnegation.

Corollary: We need not become unduly upset when others insult or mistreat us.

Showing understanding and tolerance for one's own actions and those of others is an important value in Judaism. Although Biblical Judaism is certainly replete with references to "evil-doers," rabbinical and Talmudic Judaism adopts a more nuanced view. In general, the rabbis tend to distinguish the individual's *acts* from his or her *value as a human being*. This applies both to the actions of others, and to one's own behavior. To be sure, none of this means that Judaism takes an "anything goes" attitude toward bad behavior—far from it! But a certain kind of deep human sympathy is called for, in reaching judgments about ourselves and others—a character trait known as *rahamim* (roughly translated as "compassion and mercy"). As Eugene Borowitz and Francie Schwartz (Borowitz & Schwartz, 1999, p. 68) note, the term *rahamim* shares the same root (*r-h-m*) as the Hebrew word for womb (*rehem*). The underlying implication is that the woman who nurtures her child in the womb develops an intimate and tender "relatedness" with the child. But we may read the etymological connection in a broader sense, as well: all of us are "born of woman." All human beings share both the burdens of the flesh and a destiny as mortals—for death is "the way of all flesh."

From this realization, we may come to feel a degree of *rahamim* for our fellow human beings—and for ourselves as well.

Thus, in Pirke Avot 2:18, we are told, "Do not consider yourself wicked." Rabbi Shlomo Toperoff comments on this as follows: "Self-criticism can be healthy, but self-hatred—being wicked in one's own esteem—is an unhealthy and devastating philosophy" (Toperoff, *Avot,* p. 126). Similarly, citing Rabbi Nahman of Breslov (1772-1810), Rabbi Moshe Lieber observes:

> "Rather than falling into despair over his shortcomings, [Man] must seek out positive elements in the totality of his being and judge himself favorably on that basis. Such an attitude brings one to the joy necessary to serve God." (Lieber, 1995, p. 27)

The concept that every person has inherent value is further elaborated in *Pirke Avot* 4:3, in which we are told, "Do not despise any person...for there is no person who does not have [his] hour" In understanding this teaching, Rabbi Toperoff observes as follows:

> "If you despise any man, you despise God...do not, therefore, despise the whole person even if you should discover an objectionable trait in his character. Be patient and you may yet discover that he possesses an admirable quality." (Toperoff, 1997, p. 203)

Similarly, Rabbi Reuven Bulka tells us:

> "Everything in life has its purpose, every individual has a potential meaning possibility, however distant and

remote it might seem from the superficial view. It is obligatory upon each individual to see the good and the potential of other individuals." (Bulka, 1993b, p. 146)

When we examine statements by Drs. Ellis and Harper, we are struck by how closely they parallel those of the rabbis. Thus, Ellis and Harper write:

"If human beings have any intrinsic worth or value, they have it by virtue of their mere existence, their *being*, rather than because of anything they do to "earn" it...You are "good" or "deserving" just because you are." (Ellis & Harper, 1961, p. 89)

Though the underlying premises of REBT are not derived in any direct way from theological concepts, it is interesting that Ellis and Harper cite the work of theologian Paul Tillich (author of *The Courage to Be*), in referencing the passage just quoted.

We see a similar parallelism when we analyze *Pirke Avot* 4.3 in more detail. One rendering of 4:3 is "Do not debase the entire person on the basis of a particular character flaw" (Lieber, 1995, p. 223). Lieber adds, "There is no person who does not have redeeming value, and one should never dismiss him based on one fault." This is strikingly similar to the philosophical approach to human worth taken by Ellis and Harper:

"Blaming an individual means to confuse his wrong *acts* with his sinful *being*. But no matter how many evil acts an individual performs, he cannot be intrinsically evil for the very good reason that he could, today or tomorrow, change his behavior completely and commit no additional wrong deeds...A person's (good or bad) acts are the *results* of his being, but they are never that being itself." (Ellis and Harper, 1961 p. 104, italics the authors)

This same sentiment is reflected in the writing of Nahman of Breslov, who says, "Even if one seems to have no redeeming qualities, search further. Your search will certainly uncover some bit of good which justifies the person's existence" (cited in Lieber, 1995, p. 27).

In short—while drawing on vastly different world views— the rabbinical and cognitive-behavioral perspectives may be said to converge, in the matter of the individual's intrinsic and unalienable *value.*

*****

Closely connected to the rabbis' ideas on intrinsic human value are their teachings on how we should respond to *insults or abusive speech.* It may not be obvious, at first glance, how these ideas are related. One way of understanding the link is to realize that our inherent value as human beings is not diminished because someone has insulted us. Nor is the one who has hurled the insult thereby rendered "evil" or "worthless" by such admittedly bad *behavior.* Furthermore, when we lose control or become enraged because someone has insulted us, we also lose our God-given faculty of *reason*—which, for the rabbis, is what separates us from the "lower" creatures.

Thus, in the Talmud we are told, "Happy is the person who hears himself being disdained and ignores it, for a hundred evils will pass by him [without affecting him]" (*Sanhedrin* 7A, in: ibn Chaviv, 1999, p. 596). This same idea is reflected in this passage by Ellis and Harper:

"Even when people are specifically nasty to you…it is still most important that you keep calm yourself and not condemn them severely or viciously retaliate. Whether you like it or not, they are the way they are and it is childish for you to think they shouldn't be…if you tell yourself, instead, that 'this situation stinks—tough! So it stinks,' you will at least prevent yourself from being annoyed at being annoyed." (Ellis & Harper, 1961, p. 171)

In this same spirit of self-control and composure, we find the following tale, in a commentary on the work of the Chofetz Chaim (Rabbi Yisrael Meier Kagan of Radin, 1838-1933):

"The tzaddik R' Zalman of Volozhin was traveling with R'Chaim. When they arrived at a certain inn, the innkeeper spoke harshly to them and refused to grant them a room for the night. Later, as they resumed their journey, R'Chaim noticed his brother crying. "Why are you crying?" he asked. "Did you then pay attention to the innkeeper's words? I ignored them completely!" R' Zalman replied: "Heaven forfend that I should cry over being insulted. I am crying because I sense a slight inner hurt as a result of his words. I cry that I have not yet attained the level of 'Those who are insulted…and are glad in their affliction'." (from *Sefer Toldos Adam*; cited in Finkelman & Berkowitz, 1995, p. 277)

Albert Ellis would be largely in agreement with R'Zalman's desire to abide insults with equanimity—but might have put his hand on R'Zalman's shoulder, smiled and reminded him, "Nobody has perfect control over his emotions, Rabbi!"

Principle 6: Happiness and Unhappiness are "Internally Caused"

Corollary: The world does not revolve around me, nor is the world, God, society, etc. responsible for making me happy.
Corollary: Anger and related negative emotions are irrational states that come from within and can be controlled from within.

The Judaic tradition, with great psychological acuity, posits a direct connection between ignorance (or irrational thinking) and *narcissism*. Narcissism, in turn, leads us to unhappiness, anger, and other negative emotions. Although "narcissism" has very specific meanings in the psychoanalytic literature, we may define it as the belief that, "The world revolves around me, and owes me happiness, comfort, and success." Perhaps the most forceful statement of rabbinical Judaism's views on narcissism is that of Maimonides:

> "For an ignorant man believes that the whole universe only exists for him; as if nothing else required any consideration. If, therefore, anything happens to him contrary to his expectations, he at once concludes that the whole universe is evil. If, however, he would take into consideration the whole universe, form an idea of it, and comprehend what a small portion he is of the Universe, he will find the truth."—*The Guide*

for the Perplexed, Part III, chapter 12 (Maimonides, 1956, p. 268)

In Part 3 (ch. XXIV) of his *Guide for the Perplexed*, Maimonides pursues this line of reasoning in discussing the suffering of Job. In essence, Maimonides draws a straight line between Job's *narcissism*, with its attendant *cognitive errors*, and his mental anguish (Pies, 1997). Specifically, Job errs in "imagining [God's] knowledge to be similar to ours...[and] His intention, providence, and rule similar to ours." (Maimonides, 1956, p. 303). In effect, for Maimonides, Job envisions his own needs and expectations as the *moral fulcrum of the universe*. The "principal object of the whole Book of Job," for Maimonides, is that "we should not fall into the error of imagining [God's] knowledge to be similar to ours, or His intention, providence, and rule similar to ours." When we abandon Job's anthropocentric (if not self-centered) assumption, "we shall find everything that may befall us easy to bear "(Maimonides, 1956, p. 303). As Rabbi Levi Meier puts it, Job's deficiency was not his lack of virtue but "his lack of wisdom...demonstrated by his confusion in not comprehending his afflictions" (Meier, 1988, p. 105).

In the work of Ellis and Harper, we find a similar aversion to "externalizing" unhappiness by blaming others. They write:

> "You should reject the hypothesis that human unhappiness is externally caused and that you have little or no ability to control your sorrows or rid [yourself] of your negative feelings. Instead, you should realize that most of your own misery is created by your own irrational thinking, your own self-propagandization,

and that you can eliminate most of your despair or anger by changing your thinking or your self-talk." (Ellis & Harper, 1961, p. 186)

*****

With very few exceptions, the rabbinical tradition views intense anger as a particularly egregious vice; conversely, mastering one's anger is a cardinal virtue. Indeed, Rabbi Shlomo Toperoff notes that *erekh apayim*—being *slow to anger*—is "one of the thirteen attributes of God" (Toperoff, 1997, p. 280).

As in REBT, the elimination—or at least, the mitigation—of anger by means of one's intellectual powers is a central tenet of Judaism. Furthermore, the Judaic tradition posits a direct connection between *cognitive deficits* and *anger* directed at persons or forces outside oneself. Thus, in Proverbs 19:3, we read, "A man's folly subverts his way, and his heart rages against the Lord." Similarly, Proverbs 14:29 tells us, "He who is slow to anger has great understanding, but he who has a hasty temper exalts folly" (Oxford Annotated Bible, 1962, p. 785).

The medieval poet and philosopher Solomon ibn Gabirol (ca. 1021-1058 CE) writes that. "[He] who cannot control his temper is defective in intellect." (in Sherwin and Cohen, 2001, p. 106). One can infer a "two-way street" in ibn Gabirol's formulation; that is, *defective reasoning leads to anger*, but it is also possible that *anger renders the intellect defective.* Cognitive psychologists would probably argue that a "vicious cycle" often operates in us, such that impaired reasoning leads to anger, which further impairs reasoning, which increases anger, etc.

Maimonides also stressed the destructive aspects of anger. For example, in *Hilchot Deot* (Laws of Character Traits, part of 1st book of Mishneh Torah), Maimonides counsels:

> "Anger is an extremely bad character trait, and it is proper for a man to move away from it to the other extreme and to teach himself not to become angry even over something it is proper to be angry about." (Weiss & Butterworth, 1975, p. 32)

But notwithstanding these condemnations of anger, the rabbis are also realists. Notably, *Pirkei Avot* does not admonish us, "Never get angry!" Rather, Ben Zoma urges us to be "*slow to anger*," and Rabbi Eliezer instructs us, "do not anger *easily*" (Pirke Avot 2:15). Indeed, Lieber wisely observes:

> "It is really impossible never to get angry, so the mishnah (Pirke Avot 2:15) instructs us not to anger *easily*. We must be level headed enough to assess whether the incident that sparked our anger is sufficient cause for an outburst. We should actively attempt to *find reasons* not to be angry." (Lieber, 1995, p. 106)

Similar "anti-perfectionist" ideas are propounded by practitioners of REBT. For example, Ellis and Harper note:

> "The battle against sustained psychological pain is never entirely won. When you are unhappy because of some silly idea and you analyze and eradicate this idea, it rarely stays away forever, but instead keeps recurring from time to time…[It] has to be

re-analyzed and forcibly subdued repeatedly." (Ellis and Harper, 1961, p. 72)

Principle 7: The Emptiness of Short-Range Hedonism and Immediate Gratification

Judaism in general and the rabbinic tradition in particular are not opposed to pleasure. On the contrary, in the Talmudic tractate *Kiddushin*, we are told, "A person is destined to give an accounting [before the Heavenly Tribunal] for everything he saw but did not enjoy" (Yerushalmi 4:12 (66d); Bokser, 1989, p. 174). Rather than disavowing worldly pleasure, the Judaic tradition instructs us to be *moderate* in our enjoyment, and to take our pleasures with an eye toward the *long-term consequences* of our actions. Moreover, we have it within our power to refrain from taking pleasure when doing so might harm our prudential interests. Thus, Rabbi Schneur Zalman of Liady tells us:

> "Choice, ability, and freedom are given to every man that he may act, speak and think even what is contrary to the desire of his heart...Even when the heart craves and desires a material pleasure, he [man] can steel himself and divert his attention from it altogether." (from chapter 14 of *Tanya*; in Mindel, 1973, p. 182)

Similarly, Rabbi Moshe Chaim Luzzatto (Ramchal) tells us:

> "No thinking person would exchange a momentary pleasure for long-lasting distress. All one needs to do is reflect on this, and eventually one would escape from the trap of foolish thinking." (Twerski, 1995, p. 203)

And again, from Rabbi Israel Salanter, the founder of the Mussar movement, we learn that *sekhel* (wisdom) means:

> "The capacity to perceive the consequences of human behavior…and to act in light of the consequences rather than to indulge the immediate gratification promised by a prohibited deed." (Goldberg, 1982, p. 134)

This principle is elaborated at length in the RET literature:

> "Short-range hedonism, or the insistence on immediate gratifications, is a senseless philosophy in most instances and must be surrendered for a harder-headed, longer-range approach to pleasure… You should determine what are the truly necessary activities of life—and then, no matter how unpleasant they may be…promptly perform them." (Ellis and Harper, 1961, p. 187)

Before leaving this chapter, let us summarize the seven key principles that underlie both the Judaic and cognitive-behavioral traditions:

- The need for self-awareness and self-examination
- The necessity of self-mastery
- The primacy of behavior over "insight"
- The need to cultivate self-sufficiency and equanimity
- The need to understand and tolerate the behavior of oneself and others

- The realization that happiness or unhappiness are "internally caused"
- The insight that short-range hedonism and immediate gratification are ultimately not reliable sources of self-fulfillment

Chapter 2: Biblical and Talmudic Judaism: A Brief Survey

Background

The Hebrew Bible, or *Tanakh,* is divided into *Torah* (the five books of Moses, also known as the *Pentateuch*); *Neviim* ("Prophets"); and *Ketuvim* ("Writings"). The term "Tanakh" is derived from the initial letters of these three divisions. The *Talmud*—meaning "teaching" or "study"—is often termed the "Oral Torah" and consists of the *Mishnah* and the *Gemara.* The earliest rabbis, known as the *Tannaim*, were prominent in the first and second centuries C.E., and were responsible for developing the teachings of the Mishnah. In the third century CE, Rabbi Yehuda ha Nassi (Judah the Prince) edited the Mishnah to produce the first authoritative version. The Rabbis of the 3rd-6th centuries CE, known as *Amoraim*, were responsible for developing the *Gemara,* which comprises commentary on the tractates of the Mishnah. Rabbi Judith Abrams has compared the Mishah to the U.S. Constitution, and the Gemara to the Supreme Court's process of expounding and interpreting the

Constitution (Abrams, 1991). In reality, there are *two* Talmuds: the Palestinian (*Yerushalmi*) and Babylonian (*Bavli*); however, the latter is widely regarded as the more authoritative.

Tanakh

Wisdom, knowledge, and reason are repeatedly emphasized in Tanakh. "Wisdom," however, does not mean the accumulation of data or facts about the world, or even a deep understanding of mankind, nature, or philosophy. Rather, as Rabbi David S. Shapiro observes in a seminal paper, "wisdom" in Tanakh "is synonymous with the *knowledge of God* which leads to mercy and righteousness" (Shapiro, 1971, italics added). Illustrative of this is Jeremiah's declaration:

> "Thus saith the Lord: Let not the wise man glory in his wisdom, neither let the mighty man glory in his might, let not the rich man glory in his riches; but let him that glorieth glory in this, that he *understandeth and knoweth Me*, that I am the Lord Who exercise mercy, justice, and righteousness in the earth; for in these things I delight, saith the Lord." (Jeremiah 9:22-23, italics added; King James version)

Thus, "knowledge" and "wisdom" in Tanakh have an ethical content that is inextricably linked to knowledge of God. Nevertheless, it could also be said that Tanakh places considerable value on a *cognitive process*—specifically, on the "rational faculty," as we might call it. Indeed, Rabbi Shapiro highlights the connection between *rationality* as a process, and the realization of spiritual truth:

"Through wisdom, which is the product of human reason, great things can be accomplished. *Rationality, itself a gift of God, can determine valid criteria of right and wrong.* Were the Torah to be forgotten it could be restored by the sheer power of reason. The Patriarchs observed the entire Torah before it was revealed to Israel, because, by the light of reason they had independently arrived at its truths." (Shapiro, 1971, italics added)

Given the voluminous material in Tanakh, we will focus on just three sources: the Book of Proverbs; the Book of Ecclesiastes; and the section of Tanakh known as *Neviim* ("Prophets").

Proverbs

The Book of Proverbs is the second book in *Ketuvim*, the Sacred Writings. Proverbs consists of thirty-one chapters containing wise sayings and maxims, and belongs to what is sometimes termed "the wisdom literature." Although traditionally attributed to the hand of King Solomon, Proverbs almost certainly consists of several collections of sayings from different periods in Israel's history (Jacobs, 1999).

As Prof. Ruth Sandberg has observed, Proverbs applies "...the principles of personal ethics to the practical, everyday lives of individual Jews." (lecture notes, Gratz College, 2004). Indeed, Proverbs foreshadows many of the ethical teachings we have already encountered in the Talmudic tractate *Pirke Avot* (Ethics of the Fathers).

A quick perusal of The Book of Proverbs reveals the strong emphasis on the imperatives of *learning, understanding* and *self-understanding.* It is striking that, in Book I (1.1-9.18) of Proverbs, "Wisdom" addresses the reader in the voice of a kind of prophetess, to be contrasted with "Folly." Already, we see the foundations for rational thinking in the wisdom literature of *Tanakh.* Even more striking is the proposition put forth in Proverbs 8:22-31, where we learn that Wisdom—as an aspect or activity of God—*actually precedes the other elements of God's creation.* Wisdom tells us:

> "The Lord created me at the beginning of his work, the first of his acts of old. Ages ago I was set up, at the first, before the beginning of the earth. When there were no depths, I was brought forth, when there were no springs abounding with water...When [God] established the heavens, I was there." (Proverbs 8:22-27, Oxford Annotated Bible)

The *primacy* of Wisdom is thus established both chronologically and metaphorically. Furthermore, as translator A. Cohen notes:

> "The same principles which the Creator applied in the formation of the universe have to be employed by man in the development of his highest self...[Thus] wisdom...has been appointed by God to be the controlling force of all life, both of the universe and of mankind individually and collectively." (Proverbs, 1945, p. 48)

Another link to cognitive-behavioral principles is revealed in Proverbs 8:32, when Wisdom says, "Happy are those who keep my ways." Here, we see the direct connection between wisdom and happiness—foreshadowing the cognitive-behavioral principle that *rational thinking leads to positive emotions.*

Proverbs 9:12 is particularly instructive, with respect to the idea of *personal responsibility*—a recurring theme in CBT and REBT. We are taught that "If thou art wise, thou art wise for thyself; and if thou scornest, thou alone shalt bear it." The Rev. Dr. A. Cohen—translator of the Soncino edition of Proverbs (1945)—comments as follows on this:

> "This verse teaches the doctrine of personal responsibility. Each individual has it within his power to choose wisdom and reap its reward, or to remain a scorner and incur the penalty." (Proverbs, 1945, p. 54)

It is hard to imagine a closer modern paraphrase of this teaching than the following passage from Ellis and Harper (1961, p. 131):

> "The main point…is that you are in your own saddle. You can never expect to be deliriously happy at all times in life. Freedom from all physical pain is never likely to be your lot. But an extraordinary lack of mental and emotional woe may be yours—if you think that it may be and work for what you believe in." (Ellis and Harper, 1961, p. 131)

Here is a small sampling of relevant proverbs relating to CBT and REBT (from the Oxford Annotated Bible):

12:15: The way of a fool is right in his own eyes, but a wise man listens to advice

12:16: The vexation of a fool is known at once, but the prudent man ignores an insult.

13:16 Every clever person acts with knowledge.

14:15: The simple believes everything, but the prudent looks where he is going.

14:16: A wise man is cautious and turns away from evil, but a fool throws off restraint and is careless.

14:18 The simple acquire folly, but the prudent are crowned with knowledge

14:29: He who is slow to anger has great understanding, but he who has a hasty temper exalts folly.

15:5: A fool despises his father's instruction, but he who heeds admonition is prudent.

15:32: He who ignores instruction despises himself, but he who heeds admonition gains understanding.

16:32: He who is slow to anger is better than the mighty, and he who rules his spirit than he who takes a city.

18:2: The fool does not take pleasure in understanding, but in expressing what is in his heart.

18:13 If one gives answer before he hears, it is his folly and shame.

19:3. When a man's folly brings his way to ruin, his heart rages against the Lord.

23:12: Apply your mind to instruction and your ear to words of knowledge

29:8: Scoffers set a city aflame, but wise men turn away wrath.

Perhaps of all these sayings, the one most relevant to CBT is Proverbs 19:3: "When a man's folly brings his way to ruin, his heart rages against the Lord." (In the JPS translation of Tanakh, this is rendered as, "A man's folly subverts his way, and his heart rages against the Lord."). The implication is of this is twofold: first, that it is our own foolishness that often undoes us; and second, that we tend to blame others (including God!) when we find ourselves in "ruin." One of the cardinal tenets of CBT is that we are each responsible for our own emotional and psychological well-being, and that blaming others (or God) for our misfortune is usually a self-deluding dodge. Of course, there are exceptions to this: if someone deliberately burns down your house, you may justly blame that individual for your "ruin." But CBT would hold that, even then, your *attitude* about such a calamity is still largely within your own control.

Ecclesiastes

Along with Proverbs and the Book of Job, Ecclesiastes (*Kohelet*, or The Preacher) is considered part of the Wisdom Literature. Though traditionally ascribed to King Solomon, the book was undoubtedly compiled at a much later date. *Kohelet* was originally regarded with some skepticism by the sages, since it appeared to contradict the Torah in certain respects; in particular, the sages worried about *Kohelet's* "skepticism and pessimism about the human condition." (Jacobs, 1999, p. 49). To be sure, much of Ecclesiastes reflects a kind of world-weary resignation that sees life as "vanity...and a striving after wind." (1:15). One example is Ecclesiastes 2:16: "For of the wise man as of the fool there is no enduring remembrance, seeing that in the days to come, all will have been long forgotten." Jacobs holds that Ecclesiastes was ultimately accepted because of the teaching that "shines through;" namely, "Fear God and keep His commandments" (12:13).

Notwithstanding its pessimism, there are many portions of Ecclesiastes that bear on "Learning, Understanding and Self-understanding"—the foundational principles of CBT. For example, Ecclesiastes 7:9 states, "Don't let your spirit be quickly vexed, for vexation abides in the breasts of fools." (Tanakh, 1985). This phrasing is particularly pertinent to CBT, since it implies that vexation of the spirit is something we "let happen"—and which we may also control, at least to some extent. (It is also interesting that we are admonished not to allow our spirit to become *quickly* vexed—perhaps suggesting there are times when we are entitled to become "slowly" vexed!). Similarly, in the sections on "Youth" and its transient nature (11.7-12.8), we are told, "Remove vexation from your mind, and put away pain from your body" (11:10, Oxford Annotated Bible). The implication is that although youth may be fleeting—or perhaps precisely *because* it is fleeting—we have it within our power to mitigate, or even eliminate, both mental and physical suffering. This ideal—so prominent in the Stoic tradition—is also one of the cornerstones of CBT.

Finally, Ecclesiastes 7:19 tells us, "Wisdom gives strength to the wise man more than ten rulers that are in a city." (Oxford Annotated Bible). This idea is clearly reflected in the tenets of CBT, particularly in the writings of psychologist Martin Seligman—the originator of the term, "learned optimism." As Seligman puts it:

> "Life inflicts the same setbacks and tragedies on the optimist as on the pessimist, but the optimist weathers

them better…the optimist bounces back from defeat, and…picks up and starts again." (Seligman, 1990, p. 207)

Nevi'im (The Prophets)

Nevi'im (plural of *Navi*, or prophet) comprises 21 books, divided according to length into the "Major" and "Minor" prophets. To summarize this portion of Tanakh in very broad strokes, the following may be helpful:

> "*Nevi'im* (Prophets) presents Israel's history as a nation on its land. The Israelites conquer and settle; they are beset by local enemies and eventually by imperial powers. Political and prophetic leaders vie for hearts; the supporters of God's covenant do battle against the paganism of neighboring groups and among the Israelites themselves. A kingdom, a capital, and a Temple are built and eventually destroyed. At the end of Nevi'im, prophets who experienced the exile teach a renewed monotheism to a chastened Israel." (Jewish Virtual Library)

The prophet Isaiah proclaimed his message in the period between 742-687 BC, when the Northern Kingdom of Israel was annexed to the Assyrian empire (Oxford Annotated Bible, p. 822). The southern Kingdom of Judah (including the city of Jerusalem), meanwhile, was experiencing increasing interference from the Assyrian empire; and at the same time, was being pressured by Israel and Syria to join them in an anti-Assyrian coalition. When Judah dragged its heels, there was a Syrian-Israelite invasion of Judah (Epstein, 1977). Enter the prophet Isaiah, who urged strict neutrality upon Judah, admonishing the kingdom to put its faith in God. Unfortunately, the King of Judah, Ahaz, did not pay heed to Isaiah, and actually called on Assyria for assistance! The Syrian-Israelite invasion was thereby thwarted, but at the cost of Judah's independence. It is in this tragic historical context that we find Isaiah preaching that, "My people are gone into captivity, *for want of knowledge*" (Isaiah 5:13, italics added).

Now, to repeat: the sense in which "knowledge" is used in Tanakh is far deeper than mere factual understanding. It entails "*a profound, identifying comprehension of the right relationship with God*" (OAB, p. 823, italics added). This same theme is picked up later, in the book of Hosea, where we read, "My people are destroyed for lack of knowledge; because you have rejected knowledge, I [the Lord] reject you from being a priest to me" (Hosea 4:6, Oxford Annotated Bible, p. 1091). Again, "knowledge" here means, "knowledge and teaching of God" (Oxford Annotated Bible, p. 1091).

Nevertheless, we can understand these portions of Isaiah and Hosea on another, more metaphorical level—one with important implications for the link between Judaism and CBT. Whereas the "captivity" to which Isaiah refers may be geographical and political, *each of us goes into a kind of captivity when we act from ignorance.* In cognitive-behavioral terms, we imprison ourselves, emotionally speaking, by our lack of rational thinking, understanding, and behaving. As Rabbi Raphael Pelkovitz notes with respect to Isaiah 5:13:

> "'The want of knowledge' is due to a *failure to study and pursue knowledge*" adding, "the Prophet (Isaiah)

cautions us that one will be punished for this indolence." (Pelkovitz, 1996, p. 122, italics added)

From the standpoint of the cognitive therapist, our emotional captivity is self-created, and is usually a consequence of a kind of mental and behavioral "laziness." Our habits of mind often lead us to avoid a meticulous examination of the evidence. As Ellis and Harper observe:

"Human beings easily become habituated or acclimated to what they do, even though what they do is entirely senseless and self-defeating." (Ellis and Harper, 1961, p.175)

Talmud and Related Texts

The imperatives of "Learning, Understanding and Self-understanding" are so pervasively stressed in the Talmud that it is difficult to summarize even a few of the most relevant passages (translations are from ibn Chaviv, 1999, unless otherwise noted). Thus, this section can only hint at the number of Talmudic statements relating to the knowledge, wisdom, or reasoning.

As Rabbi David Shapiro observes, "Knowledge in all its ramifications and its standard-bearers are held in great reverence by the sages of the Talmud." (Shapiro, 1971). Thus, we are told that: "A wise person surpasses even a prophet" (Bava Basra 12a). Indeed, the fourth-century (CE) sage Abbaye tells us:

"No one is considered poor except a person who lacks knowledge. In Eretz Yisrael they have a saying: If you have knowledge you have everything; if you don't have knowledge, what have you got? If you acquired knowledge, what else do you need? If you have not acquired knowledge, what good are all your possessions?" (Nedarim 40b, in ibn Chaviv, 1999, p. 408)

R. Elazar further taught:

"Great is understanding, for it was placed [in a verse] between two Divine Names, for it says, "For the God of understanding is the Lord" (1: Samuel:2:3) … [moreover]…if a person has understanding, it is as though the Sanctuary was built in his day." (Sanhedrin 89, ibn Chaviv, 1999, p. 645-46)

The Talmud emphasizes not only wisdom and understanding, but a certain kind of cognitive process—one which, in our time, we might call "rational evaluation of consequences." Thus, Rabbi Yehoshua ben Levi says:

"Whoever calculates his actions [weighing the cost of a mitzvah against its reward, and the reward of a sin against its cost] will be rewarded to see the salvation of the Holy One." (Mo'ed Katan 5a, in ibn Chaviv, 1999, p. 321)

(The "proof text" of this is Psalms 50:23: "One who orders [*vesam*] his way, I will show him the salvation of God.").

In *Pirke Avot*—the only tractate of the Talmud devoted purely to *aggadah*, or non-legal topics—we find the following:

"Hillel used to say: …One who does not increase knowledge, decreases it [and] one who does not study deserves to die." (Pirke Avot 1:13, Bulka, 1993b, p. 40). Hillel also says that, "The ignorant person cannot be pious." (Pirke Avot 2:6, Bulka, 1993b, p. 62)

Although selfless learning for the sake of getting closer to God is the Talmudic ideal (see, e.g., Pirke Avot 4:7) there are clearly "benefits" for those who study and learn Talmud. For example, "When you acquire wisdom, you will also acquire wealth, [because when you are wise, you are happy with your lot, and you feel rich (*Maharsha*)] (*Bava Batra 25b*; ibn Chaviv, op cit., p. 566).

Another benefit of wisdom, study, and understanding of the Talmud is the "protective" power conferred by such habits of mind—but only when they are *actually exercised*. Thus, we find the following vignette concerning Rabbi Chanina and R. Yonatan . The two were walking near a house of prostitution. When they approached the house, they noticed that the prostitutes withdrew. Then,

"Said one to the other, 'How did you know that our merit was so great that the prostitutes would withdraw when they saw us coming? The other replied, quoting, '[The Torah] will protect you from immorality, and *understanding will safeguard you* to rescue you from the way of evil [Proverbs 2:11,12] [and while we were walking we were discussing Torah thoughts; therefore we were protected (Rashi)].'" (Avodah Zarah 17b; in ibn Chaviv, 1999, p. 735; italics added)

Similarly, in Sotah 46b, we learn, "R. Yehoshua b. Levi said: If someone is on the road and has no companion, he should think Torah thoughts, [and they will protect him]" (Ibn Chaviv, 1999, p. 477). Study of Talmud can even protect one against the Angel of Death, as we learn in *Moed Katan 28a*:

> "The Angel of Death could not overpower R. Chisda, for he kept on studying all the time. [However] The Angel of Death climbed up and sat down on top of the cedar tree next to the *bet midrash*. The tree split [and made a loud noise], so that R. Chisda *stopped learning for a moment*. At that, the Angel of Death instantly overpowered him." (ibn Chaviv, 1999, p. 331, italics added)

This last vignette has important resonances with CBT, REBT, and related schools of cognitive psychology. It is not enough to experience a "blinding flash of insight," of the sort many people (erroneously) attribute to psychoanalysis. Rather, the cognitive therapist believes that enduring happiness and fulfillment require an almost *constant mental effort,* as Ellis and Harper note:

> "To become undisturbed...[one must]...*energetically and consistently work* at de-indoctrinating and re-indoctrinating himself." (Ellis & Harper, 1961, p. 51, italics added)

When we cease to learn, study, or seek wisdom—even for an instant, as Rabbi Chisda learned—we are no longer protected from harm. Similarly, for Ellis, *when we stop scrutinizing our own beliefs to make sure they conform to reason, we are no longer protected from mental disturbance.*

*****

Another major theme developed in the Talmud is the idea that one should not pay attention to the insults, gossip, and petty carping of others. Thus, in *Sanhedrin* 7a, we read. "Happy is the person who hears himself being disdained and ignores it, for a hundred evils will pass by him [without affecting him]." (ibn Chaviv, 1999, p. 596). Similarly, in *Shabbat* 88b, we read:

> "The Rabbis taught…People who suffer insults but do not insult others; who hear someone mocking them but don't answer; who do their duties out of love [of God] and rejoice in suffering [all humiliations that are visited on them]; of them Scripture says, 'But those that love Him are like the sun rising in full strength.'"(Judges 5:31) (ibn Chaviv, 1999, p. 104)

This faculty for "tolerating insults" is a characteristic of the secure and yet humble person. Similarly, the concept of self-restraint and "rising above the fray" is also integral to the views of Albert Ellis. Thus:

> "Even when people are specifically nasty to you…it is still most important that you keep calm yourself and not condemn them severely or viciously retaliate. Whether you like it or not, they are the way they are and it is childish for you to think they shouldn't

be…if you tell yourself, instead, that 'this situation stinks—tough! So it stinks' you will at least prevent yourself from being annoyed at being annoyed." (Ellis and Harper, 1961, p. 171)

CHAPTER 3: MEDIEVAL AND
RENAISSANCE JUDAISM (CA. 800-1600 CE)

Introduction

As Sherwin and Cohen observe, during the medieval period, the Jewish philosophical tradition "…adapted a largely cognitive approach to belief in God. Many of its advocates attempted to demonstrate belief in God on the basis of logic and reason." (Sherwin and Cohen, 2001, p. 5). As a rough approximation, this "rationalistic" stream was predominant during the 9th through 12th centuries CE. On the other hand, as Joseph Dan notes (Dan, 1996), the 13th century witnessed a countervailing trend toward *mysticism* in certain parts of Europe, as seen among the Kabbalistic rabbis of Provence (France) and Gerona (Spain). However, for obvious reasons, we will focus on the "rationalist" stream of medieval Judaism.

It is difficult to speak of medieval Jewish philosophy in this context without immediately summoning up the image of Moshe ben Maimon (Maimonides, ca. 1138-1204)—almost universally acknowledged as the greatest Jewish philosopher and Torah scholar of the middle ages, if not of all time. In many respects, Maimonides (known as *Rambam*) virtually embodied the dominant rationalist motif of the early medieval period. In the present context, we may loosely define "rationalism" as *the belief that reason is capable of leading us to religious truth; and further, that religious truth (revelation) ought to be in agreement with reason* (Guttman, 1988, p. 63).

We will have more to say about rationalism presently, in our discussion of Maimonides. However—to digress briefly—it is important to say at the outset that rationalism in the context of medieval rabbinics differs in important respects from the "rational" approach taken by cognitive-behavioral therapists such as Ellis. *Rabbinical rationalism* proceeds from certain foundational theistic and metaphysical premises that are not necessarily shared by cognitive-behavioral therapists—and definitely not by Albert Ellis! And yet, Ellis was able to find patches of "common ground" with the Rabbis. As Ellis himself wrote in response to an article on REBT and Judaism (Pies, 2000a):

> "I am not religious in any conventional sense—for I do not believe in the existence of any kind of supernatural being or god. But, as a number of rabbis, ministers and priests who use REBT have pointed out, [REBT] is in many ways "spiritual"—because it helps people to follow their existential, purposive, humanistic, and socially oriented leanings…Jewish thinking, which includes very little hell and damnation…[encourages] acceptance of human fallibility. I am happy to see that some outstanding Jewish thinkers so clearly saw this and thereby were more rational than many present-day writers!" (Ellis, 2000, p. 71)

To return now to the medieval period, it is important to note that this era is not solely the province of Rambam, though he unquestionably dominates it. Maimonides was preceded by Rabbi Se'adiah ben Yosef Gaon (ca 882-942), known as Saadia Gaon, or simply Saadia. In the opinion of Prof. Julius Guttmann, Saadia should be considered "the father of medieval Jewish philosophy of religion" and the one who first undertook "a systematic philosophical justification of Judaism."(Guttmann, 1988, p. 61). Essentially, Saadia was a rationalist in the sense described above. First, he believed that "reason is capable of reaching thorough its own powers the content of the divine truth;" furthermore, for Saadia, "The acquisition of truth by rational means is a religious precept" (Guttmann, 1988. p. 61).

Interposed between Saadia and Maimonides was another important figure in medieval Judaism—the poet and philosopher, Solomon ibn Gabirol (Hebrew: Shelomo ben Yehuda ibn Gevirol; ca. 1021-58). Gabirol is best-known as the initiator of "Jewish Neoplatonism," and the the author of *The Fountain of Life* (Latin, *Fons Vitae*). However, our interest in Gabirol is mainly with regard to his remarks on "wisdom" and emotion, and the extent to which these comments foreshadow ideas found in CBT. We shall take up Gabirol presently.

Another forerunner of Maimonidean rationalism was Bahya ibn Pakudah (Paquda), who lived from roughly 1050-1120 CE. As Sherwin and Cohen put it, for ibn Pakudah, "Faith without reason, belief devoid of cognitive understanding, is incomplete and unworthy of the truly enlightened believer" (Sherwin and Cohen, 2001, p. 5). Or, as ibn Pakudah himself stated,

"It is impossible to think that the nations would recognize us as being wise and understanding if we were not to provide infallible proofs and explanations for the truths of the Torah and our faith." (from *Duties of the Heart*, ibn Pakudah, 1996, pp. 20-21)

Indeed, while ibn Pakudah is justly famous for his emphasis on the "heart," it is clear that he placed great value on the "head." For ibn Pakudah, the *yetzer hara* (evil impulse) itself is held in check by *rationality*. Thus, in discussing the "ancient holy ones" (e.g., Abraham, Isaac, Jacob) ibn Pakudah notes that because these patriarchs were "lucid in their reasoning" and were "governed by reason," their *yetzer hara* was weak (Feldman, 2009, p. 177).

Several other figures in medieval and Renaissance Judaism whose views relate to CBT include *Rabbi Moses ben Nahman* (Nahmanides, or Ramban; 1194-1270); *Rabbi Obadiah ben Jacob Sforno* (ca 1475-1550); and *Rabbi Judah Loew ben Bezalel* (known as Maharal ca. 1512-1609). Though we will comment briefly on these three individuals, we will focus primarily on Maimonides. Finally, although it is beyond the scope of our exploration, it is worth noting that the rationalist tradition found full expression not only in Maimonides, but also in *Christian scholasticism*—particularly in St. Thomas Aquinas, who had read Maimonides with approval.

Solomon ibn Gabirol

Solomon ibn Gabirol (ca. 1021-58) has the ironic distinction of having been mistaken for a Christian Arab (known as "Avicebron") throughout the Middle Ages. His major philosophical work, *Fountain of Life*, exercised considerable influence on several medieval Christian scholastics, and it was only in the 19th century that "Avicebron" was identified as none other than Solomon ibn Gabirol! (Sherwin and Cohen, 2001, pp. 100-106). Ibn Gabirol is recognized as the author of *The Improvement of the Moral Qualities* [*Tikkun Middot ha-Nefesh*], which is considered "the first complete treatise on Jewish ethics" (Sherwin & Cohen, 2001, p. 108). Joseph Dan notes that in this treatise, ibn Gabirol "attempted to give a physiological basis to ethical preferences"—for example, linking pride with the sense of sight, and anger with the sense of smell (Dan, 1996, p. 23).

And—although there is some controversy on this point—Sherwin and Cohen conclude that ibn Gabirol was probably the author of another ethical work, entitled *Choice of Pearls* (*Mivhar ha-Peninim*). Several teachings and aphorisms in these two works are strikingly similar to the teachings of CBT and REBT; in particular, in Gabirol's emphasis on the *importance of the intellect in modulating emotion*. We also find in Gabirol the Stoic-Judaic ideas of *accepting reality; not asking too much of the world;* and *realizing one's own limitations* as a mortal creature—all of which resonate strongly with cognitive-behavioral principles. Thus we read in *Choice of Pearls*:

> "Who is the wisest of men…? He who accepts things as they come and go." (Sherwin and Cohen, 2001, p. 106)

And furthermore:

> "One whom the Creator has endowed with wisdom will not be concerned when distress and trouble occur; for

the sequel of wisdom is peace and tranquility." (from *Choice of Pearls*, Sherwin and Cohen, 2001, p. 103)

Compare this to the passage by Ellis and Harper:

"The more time and energy you expend in lamenting your sorry fate, ranting against…[those who frustrate you], and gnashing your teeth in despair, the less effective action you will be able to take in counteracting your handicaps or dealing with those who may be frustrating you…So you are deprived! Will your wailing and moaning bring back your loved one? Will your ranting at fate really make you feel better? Why not, instead, maturely accept the inevitable, however unpleasant it may be?" (Ellis & Harper, 1961, p. 113)

Also in *Choice of Pearls*, we find Gabirol repeating the theme we saw earlier in the Talmud, when "R. Chisda *stopped learning for a moment* [and]…At that [instant], the Angel of Death instantly overpowered him." (Ibn Chaviv, 1999, p. 33, italics added); i.e., one must constantly maintain one's quest for wisdom:

"A person is only wise during the time that he searches for wisdom; when he imagines he has completely attained it, he is a fool." (Sherwin and Cohen, 2001, p. 103)

Again, compare this with Ellis and Harper:

"The battle against sustained psychological pain is never entirely won. When you are unhappy because of some silly ideas and you analyze and eradicate this idea, it rarely stays away forever but instead keeps recurring...and has to be re-analyzed and forcibly subdued repeatedly." (Ellis and Harper, 1961, p. 72)

And, from ibn Gabirol's *Improvement of the Moral Qualities*, we find:

"To every man of understanding, the nobility of intellect is patent, for it is the dividing line between man and beast, in that it masters man's natural impulses and subdues passions. With the help of intelligence, man realizes the benefit of knowledge and gets to understand the true nature of things... thou wilt never see a modest man lacking intelligence, or an intelligent man devoid of modesty." (Glatzer, 1969, pp. 373-374)

Taking up what modern-day psychologists would probably call "pathological narcissism," Gabirol recounts a story about King Ardeshir, who asked a retainer to remind him, when angry, to:

"Restrain thyself, for thou art not God; thou art but a body, one part of which is on the point of consuming the other, and in a short while it will turn into the worm and dust and nothingness." (*From Improvement of Moral Qualities*, Glatzer, 1969, p. 373)

This is remarkably close in spirit to Ellis and Harper's comment:

"When you find that you are angry at or hostile to others, admit your own grandiosity and perfectionism...The thing to do…is to tackle your own grandiosity and to force yourself—yes, force yourself—to accept [the other person] the way he is, at least temporarily." (Ellis & Harper, 1961, p. 111)

Ibn Gabirol goes on to say:

"The greatest riches are contentment and patience. One of the sages has said, 'He who desires of this world only that which is sufficient for him, he will be content with the very least thereof.'" (*From Improvement of Moral Qualities*, Glatzer, 1969, p. 373)

We conclude our section on ibn Gabirol with the following cognitively-oriented aphorisms from *Choice of Pearls* (Glatzer, 1969, p. 377; Sherwin and Cohen, 2001, pp. 105-106):

"He is not clever who carefully considers a matter after he has stumbled in it, but he who comprehends it and gives it close consideration so as not to stumble."

"The summit of intellect is the perception of the possible and impossible, and submission to what is beyond [one's] power."

"Evidence of a man's mind is his choice; and his faith is not perfected until his mind has been perfected."

"It is the practice of a fool, when doing wrong, to blame others; it is the practice of the seeker of instruction to blame himself; but it is the practice of the wise and pious man [to act such that he has occasion] to blame neither himself nor others."

"[He] who cannot control his temper is defective in intellect."

*****

Nahmanides (Ramban) 1194-1270

It is easy to see Rabbi Moshe ben Nahman (Nahmanides) as an antipodal figure in medieval Jewish philosophy, standing at the "mystical" end of the spectrum, with Maimonides holding down the opposite pole of "rationalism." However, these dichotomous descriptions are misleading on several levels. (For example, one could point to certain mystical trends in some of Maimonides' writings, but that topic would take us far afield—see Bokser, 1981, pp. 73-77, for more on Maimonides' views on the mystical element of prophecy).

On the one hand, it is true that Nahmanides' world-view was richly steeped in the world of *Kabbalah*. which was "beyond logical definition, and hence beyond the grasp of dialectical thought…" (Henoch, 1998, p. 23). On the other hand, there are also elements of Nahmanides' philosophy that resonate strongly with the views of Maimonides—at least with respect to the individual's responsibility to achieve *self-mastery* and *refinement of character.* Since we are primarily interested in the relationship between thinking and feeling, we will focus on these issues, rather than on the more mystical aspects of Nahmanides' thought.

In his famous letter to his older son (*Iggeres HaRamban*), Nahmanides stresses the importance of *habit* as a way of shaping feelings. He writes:

"Get into the habit of always speaking calmly to everyone. *This will prevent you from anger,* a serious character flaw which causes people to sin....I will now explain to you how to always behave humbly. Speak gently at all times, with your head bowed, your eyes looking down to the ground and your heart focusing on Hashem. Don't look at the face of the person to whom you are speaking." (Nahmanides, Pirchei Shoshanim translation, 1996)

The preceding passage—brief though it is—suggests that Nahmanides' anticipated cognitive-behavioral theories of emotion many centuries before they were developed by Ellis, Beck, and others. As Rabbi Dr. Abraham J. Twerski observes:

"Ramban...begins with instructing [his son] to control his anger, stating that this will lead to humility, 'which is the finest of all traits.'...Ramban is conveying an important concept which has only relatively recently begun to be accepted in psychology...Conventional wisdom had been that gaining insight into the origin of the problem...would result in its alleviation... [however] many patients did indeed gain insight into and understanding of the origins of their problem, but this did not afford them any relief. More recently, behavioral schools of psychology have come to the fore, whose emphasis is primarily on changing the pathologic behavior, leaving insight to a later date. There is reason to believe that this approach is more effective…Ramban goes on to describe behavior that is conducive to humility: the way a person should walk how one should talk, etc, because these are actions one can take. If one adopts these behaviors, it is likely that they will impact on him so that he indeed begins to *feel* humble." (Twerski, 1999, pp. 206-207)

Although Nahmanides is not usually cited as a forerunner of the *Mussar movement*—which we will cover at length in Chapter 6—Ramban's letter to his son (*Iggeres HaRamban)* is "first and foremost a work of *mussar*: a practical treatise of ethics that hopes to touch the lives of its readers." (Feuer, 1989, p. vi). In addition to humility and emotional continence, *self-discipline* in the sensual-appetitive realm is also crucial to Nahamanides' ethical framework. Nahmanides uses the term "separation" to encompass what I would describe as *limiting one's desires only to those necessities that benefit body and soul* (Henoch, 1998, pp. 98-99). As Henoch points out, Ramban does not advocate a self-punishing asceticism; but rather, avoiding "what goes beyond basic necessity," regarding the needs of the body. Thus, Ramban advocates moderation in eating, sex, and other activities prone to over-indulgence—much as Maimonides before him did.

All this is quite consistent with Ellis's views on pleasure, hedonism, and moderation (though Ellis would not have followed Ramban fully on matters of sexual pleasure; e.g., in Ramban's insistence that sexual relations were solely for the purpose of fulfilling the *mitzvah* of procreation—see Henoch,

1998, p. 99). Thus, in a chapter strikingly entitled, "Acquiring Self-Discipline," Ellis and Harper write:

> "You should determine what are the truly necessary activities of life—and then…promptly perform them. Necessary life tasks usually include (a) tasks which are strictly necessary, such as eating, defecating, building a shelter from the cold, and so forth; and (b) tasks which are not strictly necessary for survival but that must be performed if one wishes to obtain desired goals. For example…commuting in order to live in the country and work in the city." (Ellis and Harper, 1961, p. 148)

With respect to hedonism, Ellis and Harper sound remarkably like Nahmanides and the rabbis of the Talmud:

> "Short-range hedonism, or the insistence on immediate gratification, is a senseless philosophy in most instances and must be surrendered for a harder-headed, longer-range approach to pleasure and enjoyment." (Ellis & Harper, 1961, p. 187)

In working with a particularly undisciplined patient, Ellis and Harper further argue that,

> "Whether you like it or not…you will not get maximum enjoyment in your work of your sex-love life until you learn to face the realities and difficulties of this world; figure out the best way of meeting—instead of avoiding—them; and act courageously and

decisively in regard to them." (Ellis and Harper, 1961, pp. 147-148)

Consistent with the ideas of *Mussar*, Ellis actually refers to his approach as a "character-building" approach to life (Ellis and Harper, 1961, p. 148). The resonance with Ramban's concept of "separation" is unmistakable.

Rabbi Obadiah ben Jacob Sforno (ca 1475-1550)

Rabbi Obadiah Sforno was truly a "Renaissance man"—physician, philosopher, Torah scholar, and confidant of churchmen and kings (Pelcovitz, 1996, p. vii). In his commentary on *Pirke Avos*, Rabbi Sforno makes several observations of relevance to CBT. For example, in commenting on Pirke Avot 3:21 ("if there is no knowledge, there is no understanding; if there is no understanding, there is no knowledge") R. Sforno observes:

> "If there is an absence of such knowledge [*da'at*], then it is due to one's *failure to toil* and fully exert one's powers of understanding [*binah*]." (Pelcovitz, 1996, p. 93, italics added)

In his own comments on R. Sforno, Rabbi Raphael Pelcovitz notes that "understanding" (*binah*) refers to "man's power of *reasoning* which refines his knowledge." (p. 93). Taken together with Rabbi Sforno's own words, it seems clear that R. Sforno is arguing that we must take responsibility for *developing our powers of reasoning and understanding,* if we are to acquire knowledge. In short, we must "work at it" if we are to develop our cognitive powers, consistent with the frequent admonition from Ellis and Harper:

> "If you have almost any habit pattern that is sabotaging your health, your happiness, or your relations with others, and you want to change it for a more effective pattern of living, you will just have to work forcefully against this habit...time and effort are the essence of human growth and development." (Ellis and Harper, 1961, p. 175)

The time and effort required includes frequent challenging of one's own "internal verbalizations" and cognitive "nonsense" (Ellis & Harper, 1961, p. 148)—but changing one's thinking alone is not enough. One must actually *undertake new, more constructive kinds of action*. Gradually, these beneficial habits will become progressively easier to perform—more nearly "second nature"—and will in turn have positive effects on one's emotions.

As Ellis and Harper note:

> "It is very difficult for the average...individual to keep fighting against his or her normal tendencies to give up easily on hard tasks...and to slacken self-discipline long before it automatically develops its own momentum and begins to maintain itself with relatively little effort. All right, so it's hard. But it still continually has to be done...Once you get going at [for example]...getting up in the morning to travel to work, your task will tend to get easier, and sometimes,

even enjoyable. But at the start, it is not usually easy; and you must not expect it to be." (Ellis & Harper, 1961, p. 149)

In commenting on Pirke Avot 4:2 ("for one mitzvah leads to another mitzvah") Rabbi Sforno suggests much the same idea. He notes not only that "one mitzvah leads to another mitzvah," but that "one sin leads to another sin." As Rabbi Pelcovitz comments on Sforno:

"Every act creates a habit, and man becomes adept at doing what he practices all the time. Hence, a mitzvah does not exist in a vacuum…but rather, brings other mitzvos in its wake. This is the greatest reward, not in the sense of payment, but in creating and developing man's character. The same is also true, unfortunately, of transgressions." (Pelcovitz, 1996, pp. 104-05)

Rabbi Sforno again endorses the idea that the individual can modify his or her "bad habits," in his commentary on Pirke Avot 5:11. This mishnah deals with "four types of temperament" as they pertain to one's tendency to become angry, versus one's capacity to be pacified. Rabbi Sforno distinguishes the individual who is *inclined* toward bad traits, from one who *possesses* bad traits. He notes, however, that "Both…have the option of correcting their attitudes, since these are natural traits which one can choose to rectify" (Pelcovitz, 1996, p. 162). This is precisely the sort of self-transformation that lies at the heart of CBT and REBT.

Finally, Rabbi Sforno's views on human value and *self-worth* are also very close to those of REBT. Thus, commenting on Pirke Avos 2.17 ("do not judge yourself to be a wicked person"), R. Sforno says:

> "If you do sin, you should realize that rectification is possible, and [you should] repent in a state of remorse over the evil [you have committed]." (Pelcovitz, 1996, p. 57)

Rabbi Pelcovitz comments further:

> "In view of mankind's frailties, a person may, in spite of all his good intentions, stumble and sin. When this occurs, he must not despair and feel that all is lost, for *teshuvah* [repentance] is always possible. The very worst thing a person can do is consider himself a… wicked person." (Pelcovitz, 1996, p. 58)

Now, to be sure: the very secular Dr. Ellis would not endorse the theological concept of "sin." However, Ellis and Harper share with R. Sforno the idea that the individual who has erred or fallen from an ideal standard of behavior (and thus, committed "wrong deeds") is *still a worthwhile and redeemable person*. Thus, they write:

> "No matter how many evil acts an individual performs, he cannot be intrinsically evil for the very good reason that he could, today or tomorrow, change his behavior completely and commit no additional wrong deeds…a person's (good or bad) acts are the results of his being but they are never that being itself." (Ellis & Harper, 1961, p. 104)

Rabbi Judah Loew ben Bezalel (ca. 1520-1609)

Rabbi Judah (or Yehuda) Loew of Prague—known as Maharal—is sometimes described as "a Kabbalist who wrote in philosophic garb." (Orthodox Union). Though perhaps best known as the creator of the *Golem*—the mythic creature that defended the Jews of Prague against anti-Semitic attacks—Maharal ought to be remembered more for his deeply spiritual, thematic interpretation of *Pirke Avos*. Rather than focus on the content of the individual *mishnayot* (teachings), Maharal considers the thematic relationships between and among these teachings (Basser, 1997, p. ix).

One of the cognitively-related concepts developed in Marharal's commentary is that of *sechel*. As Rabbi Tuvia Baser notes, *sechel* "embraces all forms and degrees of conceptual grasp, knowledge and insight." (Basser, 1997, p. xiv). Importantly, for Maharal, one is not born with *sechel*—one *acquires* it. The affinities with REBT and CBT are obvious. Regarding the intellect *(sechel)*, Maharal says:

> "The "intellect, *sechel*, is the most spiritual part of a person. The boor and the unlearned person manifest the symptoms of an undeveloped intellect. One who acts with reason can grasp the proper reverence for the Creator and will act with true piety. Therefore, [the first prescription for spiritual health is that] one should strive to acquire wisdom...[In contrast], the "spirit," *nefesh,* animates the body; it is the origin of impatience and temper. Hillel illustrates this disorder by describing one whose anger interferes with teaching Torah. This is the second prescription: *Do not be*

drawn excessively after emotions." (Basser, 1997, p. 94, italics added)

For Maharal, there is an almost Faustian dimension to *sechel,* which never remains static, but is eternally striving:

"The highest human soul is the purely intellectual spirit, *sechel nivdal.* This is the spirit that moves people to intellectual development and expression. This spirit never reaches such a state of completeness in a Jew that he could be totally at rest...[*sechel nivdal*] constantly moves to actualize itself...such continuous development and expression of the intellect is the essence of human existence." (Basser, 1997, p. 102)

Another REBT-related theme explored by Maharal is the *acceptance of suffering.* This is one of the "forty eight qualities" needed to acquire Torah, detailed in Pirke Avot 6.6. Characteristically, Maharal develops this quality in terms of the *intellect's being handicapped by excessive neediness and dependency*—themes we have taken up several times in exploring Ellis's REBT. In reference to Pirke Avot 6.6, Maharal says:

"Intellect is constrained by the physical. Only by reducing the importance of the physical aspects of life can the intellect fully develop. "Acceptance of suffering" means *reducing the constant neediness that accompanies dependence on the material things in life."* (Basser, 1997, p. 395, italics added)

This essentially Stoic teaching (Pies, 2008) is also reflected in the following passage from Ellis and Harper:

> "Almost all modern members of civilized communities (unlike, among other peoples, the ancient Spartans) seem to believe that the greater the loss is, or the more attached they are to the lost object, the more unhappy they have to be about it. Hogwash!...the unhappy person is saying to himself... 'Because I cannot have what I dearly want, this is terrible, horrible, catastrophic, and totally unfair and it just shouldn't be.'....[this] is arrant nonsense and can be objectively observed and philosophically challenged and uprooted." (Ellis & Harper, 1961, p. 118)

Similarly, Ellis and Harper write:

> "It is particularly senseless upsetting yourself because you are deprived of something you want very much. So you are deprived! ...Will your ranting at fate really make you feel better? Why not, instead, maturely accept the inevitable, however unpleasant it may be?" (Ellis & Harper, 1961, p. 113)

Similarly, both Maharal and Ellis would stress the idea of "being happy with one's lot" (another of the forty-eight traits mentioned in Pirke Avot 6.6; also see Pirke Avot 4.1). Thus, Maharal states that one who is happy with what he or she has:

> "Is one whose happiness comes from his accomplishments, and not from monetary possessions. He can

feel fulfillment because he is free of the gnawing need that comes from material dependence." (Basser, 1997. p. 397)

Similarly, in his commentary on Pirke Avot 4.1 ("Who is rich? He who is happy with his lot?") Marharal describes what he calls, "the self-sufficient personality." Such a person "appreciates what he has; and he enjoys the tranquility that comes from feeling secure and independent."

What do REBT therapists have to say about "material things"? Prof. Elliot D. Cohen, PhD—a philosopher who is also certified in REBT—provides a "rational" perspective on material possessions, based on the teachings of the philosopher Arthur Schopenhauer (1788 – 1860). Cohen describes his own experience dealing with the aftermath of two hurricanes that destroyed many of his personal possessions, and how he was able to gain perspective:

"Substantial loss of money and property is often catapulted to the status of terrible, horrible, and awful by the recipients of the loss. And, given the emphasis that popular culture places on material possessions, it is easy to see why so many of us become depressed and even suicidal over such loss. But the emotional detachment that Schopenhauer recommends is not without use even here. I have myself recently experienced substantial personal loss of property. In the fall of 2004, two hurricanes struck the east coast region of Florida where I reside...[my] house along with many of my personal possessions became infested with mold. All totaled, I lost about half my personal possessions...As I sifted through the devastation, *I made myself, at times, detach emotionally.* (It wasn't always easy)…. I do regard the destruction of my home and the loss of personal property...as bad things. But I have only to consider the recent mass devastation in new Orleans from Hurricane Katrina, or in Thailand, as a result of the tsunami. Thousands of people lost their lives. I have only to consider these natural disasters to realize just how relative the assessment of awfulness can be." (Cohen,2007, pp. 60-61, italics added)

The "emotional detachment" that Cohen describes has affinities with what Maharal describes as the *self-disciplining element of the intellect*. Thus, in commenting on Pirke Avot 4.1 ("Who is strong? He who subdues his personal inclination"), Maharal observes:

"The measure of human strength is self-discipline, which is the power of the intellect to direct the physical faculties according to what is right or wrong." (Basser, 1997, p. 214)

Finally, we have already taken note (p. 13) of the Maharal's commentary on "knowing one's place" [Pirke Avot 6:6]; i.e., this means that one must:

"Accurately assess [both] his accomplishments and his faults. If he does not evaluate himself accurately, but overestimates himself, he is in error...Conversely, if one can objectively recognize his personal faults, he will be able to recognize his shortcomings in his studies and rectify them." (Basser, 1997, p. 397)

As one trained in REBT, Elliot Cohen approaches the issue of accurate self-assessment by citing Aristotle's *Nichomachean Ethics*, to the effect that one should "assess [one's] accomplishments rationally" (Cohen, 2007, p.78). Cohen observes:

> "For [Aristotle], the most rational and rewarding form of self-assessment avoided the two extremes: vanity and mock modesty. The vain person claims greater achievements than he has actually attained. The mock-modest person disclaims his achievements or belittles them. But the virtuous person avoids both extremes by 'owning to what he has and neither more nor less.'" (Cohen, 2007, p. 78)

Moshe Ben Maimon (ca. 1138-1204)

Surprisingly, few practitioners of CBT or REBT seem aware of the affinities between cognitive-behavioral techniques and the teachings of Maimonides (Moshe ben Maimon) whose work we have already cited many times. To my knowledge, neither Ellis and Harper, nor Elliot Cohen, specifically mention Maimonides in their books. However, Cohen liberally cites *Aristotle* (Cohen, 2007), and therein may lie an important connection. As I have suggested elsewhere (Pies, 1997), Maimonides is arguably the 'father' of cognitive-behavioral therapy. Indeed, he propounded specific therapeutic techniques that bear an uncanny resemblance to those of modern-day

CBT. I believe that the affinity between Maimonides and CBT stems from the *specific philosophical-conceptual traditions* drawn upon by Maimonides and the practitioners of CBT. The Aristotelian and Stoic traditions are certainly among the most important influences on Maimonides—and, as Dr. Cohen's book suggests, on some modern-day practitioners of REBT.

Specifically, Maimonides' made direct use of Aristotle's notion of the *mean between two extreme dispositions*—though for Maimonides, this 'mean' ultimately reflected the normative dictates of the Torah. So modified, Aristotle's doctrine of the 'golden mean' became the keystone of Maimonides' clinical approach to behavioral aberrations. Maimonides' five 'faculties of the soul' *[nutritive, sensitive, imaginative, appetitive, and rational]* were also derived, in part, from Aristotle, but also from the Turkish-Arabian philosopher al-Farabi (Melber, 1968). The 'rational faculty,' or reason, was destined to play a critical role in Maimonides' philosophical and clinical thinking. It is this faculty that enables the individual to understand, reflect, acquire knowledge, and discriminate between proper and improper actions.

In his manual *Rules of Health*—dedicated to Sultan Al-Malik Alfadal—Maimonides summarized his long-held views regarding 'mental discipline.' Specifically:

> "The more mental training man has, the less affected he will be by luck or misfortune. He will not get excited over a very fortunate event and will not exaggerate its value. Likewise, if one meets disaster, he will not be disturbed and aggrieved, but will bear it valiantly." (Minkin, 1987, p. 389)

The "stoic" underpinnings of Maimonides' ethos are clearly in evidence here, as is his affinity with the teachings of CBT and REBT. Maimonides went far beyond the limited claim that our cognitions or "mental training" determine our emotions. He went so far as to say that *our very organs* are radically influenced, if not controlled, by our thoughts—essentially a presentiment of modern psychosomatic medicine. As Maimonides puts it in his *Guide for the Perplexed* (Part I, chap LXXII):

> "Man has been endowed with intellectual faculties which enable him to think, consider and act...and to control every organ of his body, causing both the principal and secondary organs to perform their respective functions." (Friedlander, 1956, p. 118)

Thus, in his *Hygiene of the Soul*, Maimonides admonishes us that, "the *thoughts* that cause heart failure because of what may possibly happen in the future must be abolished" (Savitz, 1932, p. 83, italics added). Maimonides also conceptualized asthma as a psychosomatic illness, "amenable not only to correct diet but also to spiritual treatment" (Kranzler, 1993, p. 94).

For Maimonides, as for modern practitioners of REBT, the concept of *personal responsibility* is absolutely central. As Rabbi Reuven Bulka has put it, Maimonides believes that "a human being is responsible for [his or her] behavior and cannot blame behavior aberrations on God or on any other force." (Bulka, 1993, p. 138). To be sure, Maimonides recognizes evils "which men inflict upon one another," but sees as much more numerous those evils "that are inflicted upon any individual...*by his own action*" (*Guide for the Perplexed*, Part III, chapter XI; cited in Friedlander, 1956, p. 269, italics added). Importantly, Maimonides believes that we can *avert* such self-inflicted harm and achieve happiness via concerted effort and repeated practice. Thus, in *Hilkhot Deot* [Laws of Ethics or Psychological Characteristics, 1:5,7], Maimonides describes how an individual acquires healthy, balanced dispositions:

> "Let him practice again and again the actions prompted by those dispositions which are the mean between the extremes and repeat them continually until they become easy and...no longer irksome...whoever walks in this way secures for himself happiness and blessing" (Kranzler, 1993, p. 54)

The above passage suggests that Maimonides did more than provide us with a 'philosophy' of mental health. As a physician, he was used to the *prescription* as a highly specific intervention in the treatment of physical illness. Maimonides is equally specific in his prescriptions and regimens for mental well-being. Consider his 'regulation' of the mourning process. For Maimonides—as for Freud, in his treatise, *Mourning and Melancholia*—grief can sometimes go to pathological extremes. While Maimonides clearly felt that grief was appropriate after, say, the death of a loved one, he counseled against *excessive or prolonged mourning*. Thus, in the *Mishneh Torah* [Hilkhot Avel 13:1], Maimonides advises "three days for weeping, seven days for lamenting, and thirty days for [abstaining] from cutting the hair" (Halkin & Hartman, 1985, p. 291).

More strikingly, Rambam prescribed a well-defined *behavioral procedure* for 'weaning' the mourner from the grieving process:

"During the first three days, the mourner should think of himself as if a sword is resting upon his neck; from the third to the seventh day as if it is lying in the corner; thereafter, as if it is moving toward him in the street. Reflections of this nature will put him on his mettle, he will bestir himself" (from *Hilkhot Avel* 13:12, in Halkin & Hartman, 1985, p. 292)

In effect, this is a form of 'guided imagery' not unlike that used in the treatment of various phobic and post-traumatic disorders. Like modern behaviorists, Maimonides also prescribes various forms of 'exposure' therapy, in which the feared object or situation is directly confronted by the patient or sufferer. Thus, what Maimonides [*Hilchot Deot*, chapter 1] prescribes for the excessively angry or arrogant individual is essentially a form of what we would now term 'flooding' or *in vivo* exposure:

"If one is irascible, he is directed so to govern himself that even if he is assaulted or reviled, he should not feel affronted. And in this course he is to persevere for a long time till the choleric temperament has been eradicated. If one is arrogant, he should accustom himself to endure much contumely, sit below everyone and wear old and ragged garments that bring the wearer into contempt, and so forth, till arrogance is eradicated from his heart...*If, in any of [his dispositions], he is at one extreme, he should move to the opposite extreme, and keep to it for a long time*"(Minkin, 1987, p. 396, emphasis Pies)

The last sentence describes a procedure similar to the behavioral therapist's treatment of, say, an individual with phobic anxiety about 'germs'. Using the technique known as 'flooding', the therapist might induce the patient to cover himself with dirty clothing, or touch contaminated items, until the phobic anxiety response is 'extinguished'. This is similar in nature to the approach recommended by Ellis and Harper, for an individual with a type of phobia:

> "Thus, if you are afraid to ride on buses...you must force yourself, over and over again, to keep riding on buses and to keep telling yourself, while riding, rational counterpropaganda to eradicate your irrational self-sentences. The more you do the things you are afraid of while logically parsing and contradicting your self-imposed fearfulness, the quicker and more thoroughly your needless anxieties will vanish." (Ellis & Harper, 1961, p. 141)

It may appear that Maimonides is more straight-forwardly 'behavioral' than are Ellis and Harper, in that he emphasizes *praxis* over cognition. However, in other contexts, Maimonides clearly indicates his concern with the *cognitive* component of psychopathology. Like Ellis and Harper, Maimonides (*Guide* Part I, Chap XXXI) calls attention to the 'propaganda' with which we torment ourselves, and to which we tenaciously cling:

> "We naturally like what we have been accustomed to...
> [this]...is the case with those opinions of man to which
> he has been accustomed from his youth; he likes them.
> defends them, and shuns the opposite views. This is...

one of the causes which prevent men from finding truth, and which makes them cling to their habitual opinions." (Friedlander, 1956, p. 41)

Maimonides consistently exhorts us to avoid "ideas founded on mere imagination" and to refrain from speculation based on 'false conceptions' (Friedlander, 1956, pp. 42-43). Nevertheless, to some degree, Maimonides *does* give primacy to behavior rather than to pure cognition. For him, the persistent practice of good deeds will give rise to the corresponding virtues in the individual; i.e., *there is a direct link between praxis and character.*

As we have seen several times already, REBT place great emphasis on the distinction between *needs* and *desires*. Consider this typical analysis by Ellis and Harper:

> "Adults do not really *need* the love or approval of others. In its strict definition, *need*...[means]... something that is requisite for life and happiness. Since it is quite possible for a human being to live in isolation for many years without dying or even feeling terribly unhappy...it is obvious that some persons do not *need* to be accepted by others." (Ellis & Harper, 1961, pp. 79-80)

Maimonides, too, distinguishes between necessary and unnecessary (if not frivolous) concerns, and links this distinction with personal happiness. By contemplating ethical and philosophical principles:

> "The mind becomes strong and *regards the important as important and the unimportant as unimportant.* Thus,

affects become lessened, bad thoughts disappear, fear is taken away, and the mind is cheerful, as well as the whole person." (*Hygiene of the Soul*; Savitz, 1932. p. 83, italics added)

Similarly, in the *Guide for the Perplexed* (Part III, Chapter XII), Maimonides argues:

> "Those who are ignorant and perverse in their thought are constantly in trouble and pain because they cannot get as much of the superfluous things as a certain other person possesses...all the difficulties and troubles we meet in this respect are due to the desire for superfluous things; when we seek unnecessary things, we have difficulty even in finding that which is indispensable." (Friedlander, 1956, pp. 270-271)

Finally, for all his fierce rigor and unbending discipline, Maimonides understands that we are, in the end, imperfect creatures. In the *Guide for the Perplexed*, he acknowledges that "it is impossible for man to be entirely free from error and sin" (Part 3, XXXVI; Friedlander, 1956, p. 332). Similarly, cognitive-behavioral therapists understand that nobody, no matter how disciplined, is in complete control, all of the time. Thus, Ellis and Harper note:

> "There is no point in trying to control or change *all* emotions [for example] physical pain and the unhappiness consequent to this kind of discomfort cannot always be controlled." (Ellis & Harper, 1961, p. 50)

Similarly, Cohen writes, "It is senseless for beings imperfect by nature to demand perfection." (Cohen, 2007, p. 84). Maimonides would have agreed, but might well have added, "Nonetheless, we must *strive* toward intellectual and spiritual perfection!"

CHAPTER 4:

SPINOZA AND THE ENLIGHTENMENT

Invoking the philosophy of Baruch (or Benedict) de Spinoza (1632-77) as an illustration of "Judaic" concepts poses a problem—or at least, a paradox. On the one hand, though of Portuguese-Jewish descent, Spinoza could hardly be considered a traditional or orthodox Jew. As Telushkin notes (Telushkin, 1991, pp. 212-23), Spinoza was excommunicated by the rabbis of Amsterdam because—aside from his other "heresies"—he denied the immortality of the soul and God's authorship of the Torah. So far, not so Jewish! The great scholar of Judaic philosophy, Julius Guttman, puts the matter bluntly:

> "[Spinoza's] philosophy stands in profound opposition to the Jewish religion, not only to its traditional dogmatic form, but also to its ultimate convictions… and he abandoned the attempt to reconcile this opposition through harmonization." (Guttmann, 1988, p. 265)

And yet—some have seen in Spinoza a quality of mind and spirit that is, on some level, profoundly Jewish. As D.D. Runes has put it:

> "One can say that through every thought and word of the philosopher Spinoza, there breathes the *Ruach Hakodesh*, the Spirit of Holiness of Judaism. Spinoza may rightly be called *Judaissimus*, the most Jewish of all thinkers." (Runes, 1957, p. 11)

But if Spinoza expressed the "Spirit of Holiness" of the Jews, he hardly embraced the Holy Spirit of the ancient Hebrews. To put his very complex system of metaphysics in crude terms, *Spinoza identified God with Nature,* or with the *underlying physical laws and properties of Nature*; hence, many have regarded Spinoza as a pantheist (Telushkin, 1991, pp. 212-23).

Our interest, however, does not lie in Spinoza's metaphysics, or even in his degree of "Jewishness;" but rather, in his deep-seated connection to "rational thinking" and CBT. In this realm, there can be little doubt that Spinoza shared with many other Jewish thinkers—particularly Maimonides—a profound belief in the importance of *reason and reasoning*. (Ironically, Spinoza was deeply critical of Rambam's "metaphorical" exegesis of Torah, insisting that we must take the text at face value and assess the rationality of its claims accordingly). With respect to the role of reason, Guttmann observes that for Spinoza

> "Reason is the highest power of the human soul, and all of the soul's other capacities are directed toward the embodiment and realization of reason…Only in pure

reason is the soul completely within its own realm, and is its essence fully realized." (Guttmann, 1988, p. 277)

There are two foundational principles that guide Spinoza's view of the emotions or "passions:" first, Spinoza espouses a *naturalistic* and *deterministic* view of human emotions; and second, he believes that "emotion is...*a form of thought*, in which a greater or lesser activity of the mind is expressed" (Scruton, 1999, p. 35). For Spinoza, "When a man is a prey to his emotions, he is not his own master, but lies at the mercy of fortune" (*Ethics*, Part IV, preface; translated by Elwes, 1883).

Furthermore, as Runes notes:

> "To live as the master of one's emotions and passions...
> was in the final analysis the goal of Spinoza's study in
> Ethics....living by the law of wisdom was identical
> with obedience to the divine principle." (Runes, 1957,
> p.12-13)

For Spinoza, it is our "disordered" and "confused" ideas that lead us to experience chaotic and overwhelming negative emotions; and these passions, in turn, further cloud our ability to obtain "true knowledge," in a kind of vicious circle. Thus, Spinoza writes:

> "The strong man has ever first in his thoughts that
> *all things follow from the necessity of the divine nature*;
> so that whatsoever he deems to be hurtful and evil,
> and whatsoever, accordingly, seems to him impious,

horrible, unjust, and base, *assumes that appearance owing to his own disordered, fragmentary, and confused view of the universe.* Wherefore he strives before all things to conceive things as they really are, and to remove the hindrances to true knowledge, such as are hatred, anger, envy, derision, pride, and similar emotions." (Spinoza, *Ethics*, Part IV, proposition LXXIII; trans. Elwes, 1883; italics added)

Spinoza's argument here is quite like that of Maimonides, in his psychological deconstruction of Job; i.e., for Rambam, it was Job's *inadequate understanding of the Universe* that led him to his state of self-pitying and narcissistic despair (Pies, 1997). For Spinoza, too, it is our unwillingness to accept the *underlying necessity* that governs the workings of the universe that leads us to regard things or individuals as "horrible," "unjust," etc.

Spinoza's affinities with CBT and REBT are clear, though for Ellis, "necessity" is not articulated in terms of "the divine nature;" rather, a somewhat attenuated idea of *psychological necessity* is put forward. This, in turn, greatly mitigates our (irrational) conviction that people "ought" to behave other than they actually do; or that they ought to be condemned and denigrated for their inappropriate behavior. Ellis and Harper argue:

"The idea that certain people are wicked or villainous springs from the ancient theological doctrine of free will. And although it is probably not accurate to say that man has no free choice whatever, modern psychoanalytic findings have fairly convincingly shown that he has exceptionally little free will in the sense that this term is usually employed in theological discussion…[rather] humans learn or are conditioned to behave in certain ways from their earliest childhood years…and unconsciously hold philosophies of living that drive them to follow certain behavioral pathways…[consequently] it is most difficult (although not impossible) for them to change. In these circumstances, blaming an individual for his wrongdoings is to unfairly attribute to him a perfect freedom of choice and behavior which he simply does not have." (Ellis & Harper, 1961, pp. 102-103)

For Spinoza, man's highest goal is to develop an "adequate conception of himself and of all things within the scope of his intelligence." (Spinoza, *Ethics,* Part IV, Appendix; trans. Elwes, 1883). The key to this venture is *knowledge.* By gaining knowledge and understanding of our passions, we gain control over them. Thus, for Spinoza:

"An emotion which is a passion ceases to be a passion as soon as we form a clear and distinct idea thereof… An emotion comes more under our control, and the mind is less passive in respect to it, in proportion as it is more known to us." (Spinoza, *Ethics*, Part V, Proposition III; trans. Elwes, 1883)

Thus, Spinoza insisted:

"We must strive to amend our thinking, so as to replace our inadequate and confused perceptions (which Spinoza assigns to 'imagination or opinion') with more adequate notions of reality." (Scruton, 1999, p. 22)

Furthermore, for Spinoza:

> "The rational person is the one who strives always to increase his power, to change passion to action, and to secure for himself the joy, independence and serenity that are the true marks of freedom. To achieve this condition, however, is to amend our emotions—*to master that [element] in our nature which otherwise might master us.*" (Scruton, 1999, p. 33, italics added)

The affinity with Ellis's REBT is too obvious to belabor. And, like Ellis, Spinoza recognizes *limits* to our self-understanding. We are, after all, limited creatures—for Spinoza, only God contains solely "adequate" ideas. Spinoza tells us:

> "Human power is extremely limited, and is infinitely surpassed by the power of external causes; we have not, therefore, an absolute power of shaping to our use those things which are without us. Nevertheless, we shall bear with an equal mind all that happens to us in contravention to the claims of our own advantage, so long as we are conscious, that we have done our duty, and that the power which we possess is not sufficient to enable us to protect ourselves completely" (Spinoza, *Ethics*, Part IV, Appendix XXXII, Translated by Elwes, 1883)

Nevertheless, like Ellis, Spinoza believes:

> "Everyone has the power of clearly and distinctly understanding himself and his emotions, if not absolutely, at any rate in part, and consequently of bringing it about that he should become less subject to them." (Spinoza, *Ethics*, Part V, Proposition IV; trans. Elwes, 1883)

Ellis and Harper recognize the role of Spinoza in developing what they call, "hard-headed thinking," and mention Spinoza as being among the "outstanding rational thinkers" of all time (Ellis & Harper, 1961, p. 5). Cohen specifically cites Spinoza with respect to the notion of "perfectionism"—which, as we have noted several times, is attacked as an irrational and self-defeating belief by cognitive therapists. Cohen notes:

> "I have emphasized important contributions of deterministic philosophers, such as Epictetus and Spinoza, in addressing the demand for perfection." (Cohen, 2007, p. 13)

Cohen adds that he recognizes the importance of Spinoza on this point "*without assuming the truth of determinism.*" (Cohen, 2007, p. 13, italics added). Indeed, the concept of strict determinism does pose certain conceptual problems for a therapeutic method emphasizing individual responsibility and "self-motivated" change. An exploration of such philosophical issues, however, would take us far a field (see, however, Pies, 2007 on this subject). It is enough, for our purposes, to show that both the Judaic-rationalist tradition and CBT employ determinism of a limited type to undermine "perfectionism" and moral outrage over the failings of others.

Specifically, Cohen cites Spinoza's *Ethics* as follows:

> "When [people] see something happen in Nature which does not agree with the model they have conceived of this kind of thing, they believe that nature itself has failed or sinned, and left the thing imperfect. We see, therefore, that men are accustomed to call natural things perfect or imperfect more from prejudice than from true knowledge of those things." (from *Ethics* Part IV; in Cohen, 2007, p. 36)

Cohen interprets Spinoza to be saying, "The idea of perfection is a human artifact arising as a result of turning preferences into demands," adding:

> "This is a clear reminder to see through the thin veneer of perfectionistic language of "musts" and "needs" and to realize instead your own role in imposing these demands on yourself. For example, the demand that your significant others approve of you is based on your own concept of what you deem to be a perfect interpersonal relationship...This model of human relatedness does not exist in the mind of God, in the universal order of nature, or in some supreme first principle of human relating...it is not really a necessity, not truly a "must." Changing this must to the preference that it really is can thereby help you avoid the stress you impose on yourself...Kicking and

stamping your feet…won't elevate your preference to supreme reality." (Cohen,2007, pp. 36-37)

Here we see an interesting fusion of Stoic, Judaic, and Buddhist beliefs, all under the rubric of REBT. Indeed, the sort of unreasonable "demands" that we impose upon the universe is akin to the Buddhist concept of *tanha,* which E. A. Burtt translates as "blind demandingness." Burtt describes this as that part of our nature "which leads us to ask of the universe… more than it is ready or even able to give." (Burtt, 1982, p. 28). *Tanha* is the factor "which each person is responsible for bringing under control, in order that he may be a source of true and dependable well-being to himself and to others." (Burtt, 1982, p. 28). This is virtually a synopsis of both Spinozan "rationalism" and the teachings of CBT and REBT.

Indeed, for Spinoza, as for Ellis:

> "There is implanted in every rational being the capacity to distinguish the true from the false, to weigh evidence, and to confront our world without illusions. In this capacity our dignity resides." (Scruton, 1999, p. 53)

*****

Coda: Moses Mendelssohn and the Enlightenment

No figure in Judaism is more representative of the Enlightenment era than Moses Mendelssohn (1729-86), and no figure better represents the ideal described by Guttmann as "enlightened rationalism" (Guttmann, 1988, p. 298). At the same time, on theological grounds, Mendelssohn remains a figure of some controversy within the Orthodox Jewish community, as a recent review by Zelcer makes clear (Zelcer, 2008).

Although I do not propose to draw a straight line between Mendelssohn and the ideas of CBT—so far as I know, no cognitive therapists have ever claimed Mendelssohn as a progenitor—there is a sense in which Mendelssohn is a "kindred spirit" to modern-day cognitive therapists. He shares with Albert Ellis and Elliot Cohen a kind of hard-nosed, scientific attitude that places *reason* and *hypothesis-testing* at the pinnacle of the human enterprise. Though an observant Jew, Mendelssohn propounded a "religion of reason" and insisted:

"No miracle can attest to the truth of any faith that is unable to withstand the probings of reason...Only after its rational truth had been demonstrated, is it possible, according to [Mendelssohn], to accept biblical revelation." (Guttmann, 1988, p. 295)

In Mendelssohn's own words:

"I recognize no eternal verities save those which not only can be comprehended by the human intellect but can also be *demonstrated and confirmed* by man's faculties." (from *Jerusalem*, translated by A. Jospe; in Glatzer, 1969, p. 509; italics added)

Indeed, as Zelcer observes, Mendelssohn believed that Judaism's "religious and moral principles could be logically deduced without the need of revelation." (Zelcer, 2008, p.

99). One can see a strong affinity between this "rationalizing" attitude and that of Cohen, in his book on REBT:

"Broadly speaking, a scientific approach to living means basing the answers you give to the whys and wherefores of life on rules of reporting that show you how to *rationally* arrive at and confirm your answers." (Cohen, 2007, p. 251)

Cohen is very critical of religiously-oriented thinking that is *un*critical, from a scientific standpoint:

"Do you believe that God had a hand in declaring war on Iraq? Do you think that natural disasters such as Hurricane Katrina are due to the wrath of God?...Do you put yourself through strange rituals or activities from carrying a lucky rabbit's foot to wearing a lucky garment...? Again, you are not alone. But a serious problem with subscribing to such magical powers is that it weakens your propensity for rational causal judgment." (Cohen, 2007, pp. 265-66)

There is little doubt that Mendelssohn would have been in sympathy with Cohen's line of questioning.

CHAPTER 5:
THE HASSIDIC AND CHABADIC TRADITIONS

Although we have been emphasizing the strong "rationalistic" themes of Judaism, there has always existed a more mystical and "inward-looking" dimension in Jewish thought. Indeed, well before the 18th century, there had already been something of a reaction to the rationalistic strain of Judaism. Thus, Bokser (1981) notes that the Maharal (ca. 1512-1609) "had denounced the stress on Talmudic dialectics" which he believed dulled one's "sensibility to God." (Bokser, 1981, p. 23). In the beginning of the 18th century, the mystical strain of Judaism was strengthened by a series of calamities that had befallen the European Jewish community. The massacres of Jews by Russian Cossacks under the Ukrainian, Chmielnicki (ca. 1648-1658); as well as the embrace of Islam by the supposed "messiah," Shabbetai Zvi (1626–76), each contributed to the sense that a radical, Jewish "religious renewal" was needed. *Hasidism* (or Chassidism) was such a renewal, and soon became a mass movement that led to "a veritable upheaval in the world of Judaism." (Bokser, 1981, p.

23). Hasidism was most strongly identified with the teachings of Rabbi Israel Baal Shem Tov (the Besht, 1700-1760), whose views we shall explore presently.

The 18th century also saw the emergence of a "third way" in Judaism—the movement known as *Chabad*, and identified with Rabbi Schneuer Zalman of Liady (1745-1812), known as the Alter Rebbe. As Nissan Mindel observes, Chabad was "basically a synthesis between the Kabbalah and the Halacha; between the mystical and rational currents of Jewish thought" (Mindel, 1973, p. 3). Given this rationalistic component, it is not surprising that Rabbi Zalman's philosophy shows a number of affinities with certain principles of CBT. More surprisingly, we can find rationalistic tendencies *even within Hasidism proper*—though not in the scientific-empirical sense of "rationalistic" discussed in connection with Mendelssohn and the spirit of the Enlightenment. Rather, the "rational" elements within Hasidism—and much more prominently, in Chabad—have to do with the *mastery of primitive emotions and urges, under the aegis and influence of higher-level cognition.* Indeed, there is an intriguing distinction that appears in the writing of the Chassidic rebbe, R'Henoch of Alexander (Stern, 1999, p. 427). The term *chassid yashar* (roughly, "upright pious one") refers to:

"A rational–acting *chassid* who carefully considers his behavior. This is in contrast to a *chassid shoteh,* whose piety leads to foolish, albeit sincerely intentioned deeds." (Stern, 1999, p. 427)

In this chapter, we will focus primarily on the teachings of the Baal Shem Tov; Rabbi Nahman (Nachman) of Bratslav;

Rabbi Schneuer Zalman; and Rabbi Yehudah Aryeh Leib Alter (*Sfas Emes*). Taken together, these rebbeim arguably represent the tradition of the *chassid yashar*.

Baal Shem Tov

Israel ben Eliezer Ba'al Shem Tov (1700-1760)—usually known by the acronym, the "Besht"—is a figure more of colorful legend than of settled history (Bokser, 1981, p. 177). Though schooled in traditional rabbinical Judaism, the Besht "discovered inner meanings in the classic texts themselves, and their hidden, immanent light shone brightly for him" (Bokser, 1981, p. 177).

Insofar as these mystical leanings dominated the life and thought of the Besht, it is somewhat surprising to discover a number of "rationalist" elements in his thinking. Indeed, in the broad sense of the term "rational" that we have described in connection with CBT, the Besht shows certain affinities with Ellis, Beck, and modern cognitive therapists. This conclusion must be greatly tempered by the fact that the Besht himself left no writings of his own—we have only the quotations, tales and aphorisms preserved by the Besht's disciples and interpreters (such as Martin Buber) on which to base our conclusions. Even the "Will of the Besht" cited here is apparently one of several versions; nevertheless, Bokser considers it as comprising "the basic teachings of Hasidism" (Bokser, 1981, p. 178). Thus, when we allude to "the views of the Baal Shem Tov," we are really describing these foundational Hasidic teachings. The first rationalist element we find in the Besht's will is the very general –but crucially important—claim that *one's emotional state is strongly influenced by one's outlook* or frame of reference. Thus, the Besht observes:

"Whatever may happen [to the individual], whether people praise him or disparage him, it should be all the same to him, and similarly with reference to all other matters...no matter what happens, let him say: This surely emanated from God, and if it is agreeable to Him it is agreeable to me." (Bokser, 1981, p. 179)

This is obviously a theocentric framework, not shared by REBT; but the implication is that one's *cognitive schema* of what is happening can determine one's emotional response. That is, if one can view what happens in life as emanating from God, one can maintain a state of "agreeable" equanimity, even in the face of life's misfortunes. Indeed, the Besht's statement is reminiscent of classical Stoic beliefs, which also have much in common with rabbinical Judaism (Pies, 2008).

Similarly, Jacob Yuroh Teshima, writing on the affinities between Zen Buddhism and Hasidism, has this to say about the latter:

"[Hasidism's] main policy was to *accept reality as it is*, no matter how deteriorated from the ideal situation, and to find its positive aspect in order eventually to sublimate the entire reality...A Zaddik of Hasidism... enriches his life by reversing a negative into a positive value." (Teshima, 1995, p. 69, italics added)

In cognitive-behavioral terms, this mental habit is called "reframing." For example, the business executive who loses her job during the recession may see, in this admittedly painful loss, an opportunity to pursue her life-long dream of becoming a writer. Cognitive therapist Elliot Cohen cites the existential philosopher Jean-Paul Sartre as an exemplar of this very "Hasidic" point of view: existentialism holds that *we are free to choose the meaning we wish to attach to any given event.* Cohen summarizes this view as follows:

> "Take responsibility for your interpretation of life signs and omens. Instead of ascribing self-destructive, negative meanings to the events in your life, invent life-affirming, constructive ones." (Cohen, 2007, p. 145)

But Hasidism does not stop at affirming the control we have over our "interpretations" of life. The Besht also espouses the view that *man has control over his more primitive feelings and impulses*—a central principle of RET and CBT, as we have repeatedly seen. Thus, the Besht teaches:

> "If [a man] should find himself drawn toward anger, which is a form of evil [and] fear, deriving from the attribute of sternness, *let him overcome his impulse*, and fashion out of this attribute a vehicle for the service of God." (Bokser, 1981, p. 181, italics mine)

Similarly, the Besht prescribes a form of what Ellis or Beck would call, "rational self-talk," in the face of depression—though for the Besht, one is addressing one's "evil impulse:"

> "Sometimes the *yezer hara* [evil impulse] deceives a man by telling him that he committed a grave sin, whereas he only performed a minor infraction, or no sin at all. The intention of the *yezer hara* is to lead the person to a state of depression...it is well that a person

be wise to this deception and tell the *yezer hara*: I will not be disturbed by this infraction about which you pursue me…and even if what I did is in some respects sinful, it will be more agreeable to my Creator that I do not allow myself to be disturbed over my infraction… even if I do not perturb myself over the infraction… God will not be angry with me…This is the general principle in serving the Creator, that a person guard against being depressed, to whatever extend he can… *this is how one must condition himself in looking at things.*" (Bokser, 1981, pp. 182-83; italics mine)

If we substitute the phrase "one's own internalized irrational ideas" for "the *yezer hara*," we have a rough approximation of REBT's central teachings. The individual, using the techniques of REBT, "tells" these "internalized irrational ideas" that they cannot disturb him or her. Thus, the primacy of the individual's ideas and will are evident in both Hasidism and RET. Also note the element of "conditioning" or self-training expressed by the Besht—a fundamental tenet of cognitive-behavioral therapy.

Nahman of Bratslav

Rabbi Nahman of Bratslav (1772-1810)—a great-grandson of the Besht—has rightly been termed, by Arthur Green, "The Tormented Master" (Green, 1981). As Nahman's biographer, Green notes that, "The most essential religious reality for Nahman was always the realm of his own inner struggle." (Green, 1981,p. 40). Indeed, in a letter written to his own disciples, Nahman alluded to his struggle against "the very jaws of the wicked Samael" who had "[gnashed] his teeth at me." [*Hayyey MoHaRaN* 6, cited in Green, 1981, p. 229].

And yet, we need to examine a striking paradox in a man whom Green describes as "a deep and thoroughgoing anti-rationalist"(Green, 1981, p. 298). On the one hand, it is true that for Nahman, the essence of religion is *faith*, not reason or logic. And yet—Nahman's "penchant for paradoxical thinking" is also recognized by Green. Despite his espousal of "simple faith" (*emunah*), Nahman also tells us:

> "The *primary essence of man is his comprehension, and wherever one's reason is focused, there one has his being...* whatever deficiencies a person suffers...they all stem from a lack of knowledge... The basis of deficiency or perfection is the absence or presence [respectively] of knowledge...Similarly, anger and cruelty result from a lack of comprehension, as it is written (Eccl. 7:9), "Anger abides in the bosom of fools...." In the hereafter, *comprehension will be diffused*, and all will know God...and therefore there will be an end to anger." (*Liqqutei Moharan* 21; italics added; cited in Bokser, 1981, pp. 241-242)

And in the realm of emotion—particularly when it came to the crushing bouts of depression he suffered—Nahman is surprisingly "rational." As Green puts it, in Nahman's later years, he:

> "Is not going to let his illness get the best of him. The threat of depression is a real one...He seeks to escape it by reasserting his own ability to maintain

willful control over his own mind. He contrasts himself with those who "do nothing to help themselves," who do not work to fight off the depression that engulfs them." (Green, 1981, p. 245; italics added)

Nahman was acutely aware of some of the same human foibles and "hang-ups" that cognitive therapists often point out. As Bokser puts it, Nahman believed:

"Trivialities disturb [the average person]; he focuses on the negative side of everything and sees himself as well as his fellow humans in a harsh light. People are like beautiful flowers which have not blossomed; the best part of their natures [is] dormant." (Bokser, 1981, p. 228)

And what is the cause of man's existential predicament? For Nahman, as for the cognitive therapist, there is an essentially *cognitive* etiology. Nahman himself tells us that "The reason why people remain far from God is that *their minds are not settled.* They do nothing to help themselves in this regard"(*Liqqutim* II 10, italics added; cited in Green, 1981, p. 244). Nahman argues, "The only real poverty is a poverty of enlightenment" (Bokser, 1981, p. 234), and goes on to discuss what he calls "contraction of the mind." He writes:

"There are times when…a person is without wisdom, and this is represented in what we call a "contraction of the mind…." [To deal with this]…he must endeavor to strengthen himself to reach an "expansion of the mind." On attaining an "expansion of the mind," all the severities of God's judgment are nullified and one experiences God's kindness and mercy…a person must continually renew his mind…for the renewal of the mind is the renewal of the soul; the mind is the soul." (Bokser, 1981, p. 234)

How, for example, can we "renew" our minds when we have feelings of self-loathing or inferiority—undoubtedly, feelings Nahman himself experienced all too frequently? Nahman's counsel is strikingly similar to that of modern-day cognitive-behavioral therapists. Nahman tells us:

"Rather than falling into despair over his shortcomings, [Man] must seek out positive elements in the totality of his being and judge himself favorably on that basis. Such an attitude brings one to the joy necessary to serve God." [*Liqqutei Moharan* 282, cited in Lieber, 1995, p. 27).]

Note that Nahman's advice is fundamentally *cognitive* and *rational*: our self-esteem and mood are dependent upon *judgment and attitude*. To be sure, we may draw close to G-d by means of simple faith and the "setting aside" of intellect. *But we surmount our own despair by thinking our way out of it,* thereby leading ourselves to *joy*. Nahman's advice on judging ourselves and others is strikingly similar to statements we have seen from Ellis and other cognitive therapists. Nahman says:

"One must judge each person favorably…one must seek out some good in him, wherein he is not wicked… one must similarly find some good in oneself…if a person, on confronting himself, should find that there is nothing good in him, that he is full of sin, and the evil impulse conspires to defeat him as a result of this by inducing in him depression and melancholy, he must not allow himself to be defeated by this. He must seek and find some good in himself, for how is it possible that he has not performed some commandment or some good deed in the course of his life?" (Bokser, 1981, p. 236-7)

The last portion of this passage easily could serve as a retrospective "bookend" to the *prospective* view of human worth propounded by Ellis and Harper; i.e.:

"No matter how many evil acts an individual performs he cannot be intrinsically evil for the very good reason that he could, today or tomorrow, change his behavior completely and commit no additional wrong deeds." (Ellis and Harper, 1961, p. 104-105)

Shneur Zalman of Lyady

Rabbi Shneur Zalman (1745-1813) was a contemporary of Rabbi Nahman. His magnum opus, the *Tanya* (*Sefer Shel Beinonim*) has formed the basis of the *Habad* (*Chabad*) or Lubavitch movement (Bokser, 1981, p. 210). One could say that Rabbi Shneur Zalman (RSZ) occupies a point almost equidistant from the mystical and rational poles of Judaism. On the one hand, we find in RSZ's writings many references to "the soul's yearning to cleave to God" [*Iggeret haKodesh* 18], "the return of the soul to its divine source" [*Tanya* 26], and many other ideas found in the Jewish mystical tradition (Bokser, 1981, pp. 218-219). But on the other hand, we find that RSZ developed his own strain of Hasidic thought that incorporated *strong rationalist elements*. For example, RSZ modified the concept of the *zaddik* (the righteous or saintly individual), so that it was seen "in terms closer to the classic conception of the rabbi as a teacher and a guide, but not as a channel of divine grace." (Bokser, 1981p. 210).

RSZ's "psychology" is complex, and we can provide only a brief synopsis here. Essentially, he sees man as possessing both an "animal soul" (*nefesh ha-behemith*) and a "divine" soul. The latter consists of three parts or levels of development, of which the *neshamah* is the highest portion and emanates directly from God. The divine soul also generates three "intellectual faculties:" *Chochmah* [*Hokhmah*] or wisdom; *Binah*, or understanding; and *Da'at [Da'ath]*, or knowledge. ("Chabad" is an acronym derived from these three terms). As Teshuma summarizes RSZ's psychology, "He taught how to overcome the force of the animal soul by the unified force of *Hokhmah, Binah,* and *Da'ath*" (Teshuma, 1995, p. 118).

The concept of *da'at* is particularly important, since it:

> "Represents the final state in the mental process, where the idea attains its most definite comprehension, which, in turn, *gives rise to corresponding emotions and feelings.*" (Mindel, 1973, p. 33, italics mine)

Here we see the notion that emotions and feelings *arise from the ideas we form* in the "pathway" from *chochma* (where an idea is first conceived) to *binah* (where the idea is analyzed) to *da'at* (where the idea is fully realized). Teshuma makes a further point:

> "It is impossible for a person to express a *proper emotion* without an exact *knowledge* of his circumstances," (Teshuma, 1995, p. 118, italics added)

In some ways, this notion of expressing a "proper emotion" is reminiscent of Spinoza's concept of how we overcome "passions" (passive emotions), which stem from *confused or inadequate ideas*. For Spinoza—as perhaps for RSZ—"the source of our strength against the passions lies in knowledge" (Steinberg, 2000, p. 66).

In his spiritual practice, RSZ can certainly sound quite "mystical," emphasizing intense catharsis and penitence. Thus, Foxbrunner tells us that Zalman advocated:

> "Weekly or monthly periods of introspection and self-berating that, ideally, were to culminate in a tearful outpouring of the heart. This weeping was intended simultaneously to purge the soul of its spiritual guilt and of all its worldly worries; it would then be capable of serving God with unadulterated joy." (Foxbrunner, 1992, p. 115)

Perhaps RSZ had the same intuition as Spinoza; namely, that we can't eliminate one strong emotion by reason alone; rather, we need the catalyst of a strong, *countervailing* emotion or affect (Steinberg, 2000, p. 61). And yet, RSZ paid high tribute to the role of the intellect. This is especially true in his depiction of the struggle between the "divine soul" and the "animal nature" inherent in all human beings. Thus, Foxbrunner tells us:

> "It is clear that in *Tanya* (and in some discourses) *the emotions are generally caused and completely controlled by the intellect.* A mind engaged in contemplating sublime matters will eventually bring forth sublime emotions. Conversely, the powerful, untamed physical passions generated by the animal soul may always be tamed and sublimated by the intellect of its divine adversary." (Foxbrunner, 1992, p. 102, italics added)

Indeed, in Tanya (chapter 12), RSZ writes:

> "As soon as there rises from his [the *beinoni*, or "intermediate" person] heart to his mind some animosity or hatred, God forbid, or jealousy or anger....*his mind exercises its authority and power over the spirit in his heart*, to do the very opposite and to conduct himself towards his fellow with the quality of kindness." [*Tanya* 12, section 8, italics added; translation from Steinsaltz, 2003, p. 286]

But RSZ's concept of the emotions does not necessarily pit them against the intellect. His view is far more subtle than that. In certain instances, the intellect or rational faculty actually gives rise to intense emotion, albeit of an exalted type. Thus, in *Tanya* (chapter 3), RSZ tells us:

> "When the intellect in the rational soul deeply contemplate and immerses itself exceedingly in the

greatness of God…there will be born and aroused in his mind and thought the emotion of exalted awe… his heart will glow with an intense love like burning coals…with craving…towards the greatness of the Blessed Infinite." (Steinsaltz 2003. p. 97)

Thus, the rational and emotive faculties are not necessarily adversaries, so long as the object of the intellect is "the greatness of God." Indeed, for RSZ, love associated with God's greatness is intimately linked with *exercise of the intellect*. In the *Tanya*, RSZ describes *ahavat olam* as "the Love arising from contemplation of God's greatness and the concomitant realization that He is the Source of all pleasure" (Foxbrunner, 1992, p. 179). *Ahavat olam* originates in the divine soul, and is "commensurate with the knowledge of God one attains… [and thus] varies according to the *power and application of one's intellect*" (Foxbrunner, 1992. p. 179, italics added).

This is quite reminiscent of Rambam's teaching, in *The Guide for the Perplexed*, that one's love of God is fundamentally connected to one's *intellectual capacity*. Thus, Maimonides refers to "the perfection of those ideas that lead [one] to an intense love of God." (Maimonides, 1956, p. 390). For Maimonides, as "man's intellect increase[s] in strength," so does "his love for the object of his knowledge"—namely, God. For sages like Moses who attain such knowledge of God, even death becomes an act of divine love: "nothing but a kiss." (*Guide* Part III, chapter LI; Maimonides, 1956, p. 390).

There is yet another link between RSZ's methods and those of CBT. Foxbrunner points out that the kabbalistic term *birur* is applied by Rabbi Zalman to the study of the Oral Torah:

"Study of the Oral Torah…is essentially an intellectual act. In kabbalistic terms, it is an act of *birur*—sifting, separating, and selecting the good from the evil, the permissible and desirable from the prohibited and undesirable. And, according to the *Zohar*, the faculty that performs *birur* is the intellect…Everything must therefore be scrutinized…to discern (halikhically) whether or not the entity, emotion, or act in question contains a redeemable element of goodness." (Foxbrunner, 1992, p.159)

Although on the face of it, this kabbalistic process would seem to have little in common with cognitive behavioral therapy, the "deep structure" of CBT and the process of *birur* are not dissimilar. In RET, for example, the patient is taught to *sift, separate, and scrutinize* emotions and behaviors. Thus, Ellis & Harper (1961, p.24) see rational thinking as a "reflective kind of discrimination." For them, negative emotions may be attacked and changed "by parsing the thoughts and emotions into the essential sentences of which they consist and then changing these sentences" (Ellis & Harper, 1961, p. 28).

This intellectual aspect of kabbalistic thinking may seem surprising in light of its "mystical" aura. But as Louis Jacobs explains:

"The state in which God's presence is acutely felt…is known as that of *gadlut* ("greatness"). The opposite state….is known as *katnut* ("smallness"). It must, however, be appreciated that these terms are taken from the Kabbalah and have a meaning based on the kabbalistic system. Here the terms in full are respectively: *gadlut de-mohin* ("greatness of the brains") and *katnut de-mohin* ("*Smallness of the brains*")...When the "brains" are much in evidence... there is *gadlut de-mohin*." (Jacobs, 1977, pp. 13-14)

*****

Like Rabbi Nahman and other Hasidic masters, Rabbi Shneur Zalman seems to have been concerned with combating serious depression. RSZ distinguished between what he called "dejection"—what modern-day psychiatrists might term, "major depression"—and "bitterness." Whereas dejection is a crippling emotion that "inhibits service" bitterness is a form of "active dissatisfaction" with one's shortcomings (Foxbrunner, 1992, p. 122). Bitterness, in this sense, is a kind of *goad to self-improvement*. It is not unlike the modern cognitive psychologist's instruction to the depressed patient; e.g., "Write down all the things that you'd like to change about yourself, and then some practical ways you might bring that about." This instruction is provided in a context that also emphasizes self-acceptance—distinguishing the individual's self-defeating actions from his or her ultimate value as a human being (5).

Similarly, Foxbrunner writes that "RSZ devotes much attention to psychological strategies for dealing with periodic depression. These episodes were to be examined and their nature determined" (Foxbrunner, 1992, p. 120). Then, the individual could begin to alter his thinking so as to alleviate the depression. For example:

"Sadness arising from one's apparent spiritual weakness—the inability to suppress profane thoughts, for example—could be overcome by simply accepting one's lot...as one of the vast majority of men whose purpose in life is constantly to struggle with profane thoughts, speech, and actions naturally arising from the animal soul and the *yetser hara* [evil impulse]." (Foxbrunner, 1992, p. 120)

In effect, Zalman is advocating self-acceptance and the avoidance of unrealistic, perfectionistic thinking. "Accepting one's lot" also carries with it a strong element of Stoicism. Rabbi Zalman is describing essentially a *change in one's belief system*, though it occurs in the hothouse atmosphere of "self-abasement and self-effacement" sessions (Foxbrunner, 1992, p. 121). These are akin to what the narcissistic individual undergoes—often painfully—as his grandiosity and self-involvement are gradually confronted in psychotherapy.

Finally, Rabbi Zalman affirms a basic teaching of CBT; namely, that we have the ability to overcome our short-range, hedonistic impulses. In particular:

"The choice, ability, and freedom are given to every man that he may act, speak and think even what is contrary to the desire of his heart...Even when the heart craves and desires a material pleasure, he [man] can steel himself and divert his attention from it altogether." (*Tanya*, chapter 14, cited in Mindel, 1973, p. 182)

Compare this with Ellis and Harper:

"Short-range hedonism, or the insistence on immediate gratifications, is a senseless philosophy in most instances and must be surrendered for a harder-headed, longer-range approach to pleasure… You should determine what are the truly necessary activities of life—and then, no matter how unpleasant they may be…promptly perform them." (Ellis and Harper, 1961, p. 187)

Rabbi Yehudah Aryeh Leib Alter (the *Sfas Emes,* 1847-1905) and Other Hasidic Masters

Rabbi Yehudah Aryeh Leib Alter (1847-1905)—usually known as *Sfas Emes* ("Lips of truth")—represents the culmination of ten generations of Chassidic tradition, beginning with the Baal Shem Tov (Stern, 1999, p. xv). The thoughts of the *Sfas Emes* and other Chassidic *rebbeim* are presented by Rabbi Yosef Stern, in a commentary on *Pirke Avot*, and this is the primary source for our discussion. What is perhaps most remarkable (though not really surprising) is the strong "rationalist" tendency in the thinking of the *Sfas Emes* and several of the other Chassidic masters whose teachings are discussed by Rabbi Stern. In contrast to the stereotype of the ethereal or unworldly "mystic," the tradition of the *Sfas Emes* and his progenitors strikes the non-Chassidic reader as pragmatic, hard-nosed, and "no-nonsense" in its approach to life—features one immediately associates with the figure of Albert Ellis! Notwithstanding obvious theological differences with the Chassidic tradition, CBT and RET would readily understand the *Sfas Emes*'s positions on a number of psychological and behavioral matters. At the same time, many of the *Sfas Emes*'s comments on *Pirke Avot* reflect a subtle and many-layered understanding that is anything but "concrete."

For example, in Pirke Avot 1:6, we are told, "Appoint a Torah teacher (*rav*) for yourself." Conventionally, a "Torah teacher" would refer to a rebbe or rabbi. However, citing the *Sfas Emes*, Rabbi Stern offers an alternative interpretation:

> "The term [*rav*], which can also be defined as master, refers to oneself rather than to an external master. Master yourself! Control yourself so that your every action reflects the Torah and its values." (Stern, 1999, p. 33)

The emphasis on self-mastery and self-control is, of course, a theme we have explored many times in the writings of Ellis, Beck, and cognitive therapists. This is made explicit in Rabbi Stern's psychologically astute interpretation of *Pirke Avot* 1:14—Hillel's famous teaching that begins, "If I am not for myself, who will be for me?" (Stern writes under the heading, "Never Lose Your Head," which could easily sum up most of CBT and RET). Citing the Chassidic rabbi, R'Chanoch Henach of Alexander, Stern relates a parable regarding a "hopelessly disorganized fool" who makes the following list prior to going to bed: "My clothing is hanging in the closet, my shoes are beside my bed, and my head is in my bed, under the covers." The next morning, the fool awakens to find his clothing and shoes, but not his head! Rabbi Stern draws the following moral from the story:

> "It is not sufficient for peripheral matters to be in place, unless my head, the core of all my thoughts and actions, is also in place (*Maggidei HaEmes*). In this light, we may gain new insight into the *mishnah*'s

teaching ["If I am not for myself, who will be for me?"].
If I can't find myself…how can I locate anything else?"
(Stern, 1999, p. 52)

The Chassidic masters also suggest that this entity we call "myself" is a kind of work in progress—and not something that should be "written off" prematurely, from the standpoint of moral improvement. In commenting on *Pirke Avot* 2.21 ("You are not required to complete the task, yet you are not free to withdraw from it"), Rabbi Stern sums up what might be characterized as the Chassidic perspective on self-improvement:

"From this mishnah [2:21], we can infer an extremely vital principle—that it is never too late to change the moral course of one's life. If indeed we were obligated to *complete* our mission, then one might rationalize that it is already too late. But since we only need to *commence* it, then it is never too late in life to at least begin." (Stern, 1999, p. 150)

Indeed, in the Chassidic tradition:

"A residue of the Divine Presence…is embedded in each of us, even in the evildoers…Even the evildoer, since he is never fully detached from [God], can build on his inner spiritual core and eventually find his way back to [God]." (Stern, 1999, p. 246, adapted from *Sfas Emes*)

The image of the Divine "residue" in each of us is reminiscent of the Lurianic concept of the "holy sparks," which are trapped within even the lowliest of material entities—and which can be "released" with sufficient effort. Similarly, the evildoer can build upon the "residue of the Divine Presence" within, and change his character. This view of self-improvement—and self-redemption— is largely consistent with the views of Ellis and Harper:

> "Accept your own and others' wrongdoings objectively and unmoralistically: as misdeeds *to learn from and to correct* in the future…when you blame yourself…you are being perfectionistic and grandiose, and…you are thereby invariably helping to perpetuate rather than correct your…misdeeds. *Never confuse an individual with his acts, a person who acts badly with a bad person.*" (Ellis & Harper, 1961, p. 186, italics added).

For Ellis, as for the Chassidic *rebbeim*, the journey of the self involves *introspection and self-probing*. As Ellis and Harper put it:

> "The job of the neurotic is to *uncover* and understand the basic unrealistic ideas with which he is disturbing himself…[and] to change the notions which lie behind and keep creating his disturbance." (Ellis & Harper, 1961, p. 51, italics added)

The image of "uncovering" proves to be relevant to the Chassidic view of personal growth, as well. In his discussion of the *Sfas Emes*, Stern discusses the Biblical account of Abraham "digging wells and removing the earth from wells that had been sealed." (Stern, 1999, p. 154). This part of Genesis (21:25-31) deals with a dispute between Abraham and Abimelech over the latter's seizure of a well that Abraham had dug. As Rabbi Stern observes:

> "We find him [Abraham] digging wells and removing the earth from wells that had been sealed. By doing so, he demonstrated his determination to reach the wellsprings of his own *neshamah* [the highest portion of the divine soul] by removing all the impediments to his growth." (Stern, 1999, p. 154)

Removing earth from the sealed wells is emblematic of the method, in REBT, of uncovering irrational ideas—which are seen as "impediments to growth." Interestingly, whereas several translations of Genesis 21:25 state, "When Abraham *complained to* [or "reproached"—Tanakh, p. 30] Abimelech about a well of water which Abimelech's servants had seized" (Oxford Annotated Bible, p. 25), Young's Literal Translation gives the following wording:

> "And Abraham *reasoned* with Abimelech concerning the matter of a well of water which Abimelech's servants have taken violently away." (http://yltbible.com/genesis/21.htm)

The ambiguity of translation lies in the Hebrew word, *yakach,* which appears to have a very broad range of meanings (e.g., "rebuke," "correct" "reason" "convince," etc.), according to some sources (next.bible.org/lexicon). But if we accept Rabbi Stern's interpretation of the "wells" parable in Genesis 21:25— i.e., Abraham was one who tried to "reach the wellsprings of his own *neshamah*"—then it makes sense that Abraham would attempt to "reason" with Abimelech. The individual who looks deeply into his own soul is, in other words, more likely to discern the predicaments and needs of others—and thereby to offer reasoned arguments to persuade the other. In effect, self-mastery (Stern, 1999, p. 33), self-knowledge and reasoning with others are all part of the same spiritual—and, I would suggest, cognitive-behavioral—"package."

It is intriguing that philosopher and rational-emotive therapist Dr. Elliot D. Cohen uses the metaphor of "poisoning the well" in his discussion of "empowering others" (Cohen, 2007, pp. 159-63):

> "In advising someone, you leave it open for the person to decide what to do. In advising someone, you guide them. By poisoning the well, you goad them. Advising depends on rational argument…in contrast, by poisoning the well, you manipulate and control others for self-serving purposes in the guise of advice." (Cohen, 2007, p. 162)

In essence, Abimelech's seizure of one of Abraham's well was an act of manipulation and control—an expression of *anti*-reason. In contrast, Abraham's attempt to reason with Abimelech was an act of rational argument—and thus, an affirmation of non-manipulative reason. It is tempting to draw the further conclusion that—had Abraham not been a man willing to look into his own soul by "uncovering the well"—he would not have had the moral and spiritual capacity to rebuke, correct, or reason with Abimelech.

*****

Self-acceptance is, of course, a foundational principle of CBT and REBT. In an importance sense, this concept is shared with Chassidic Judaism. That said, as we shall see in our discussion of the *Mussar* movement, self-acceptance must not be confused with *self-complacency* or "smugness" (Stern, 1999, p. 266), when it comes to improving oneself and one's ethical development.

Chassidic Judaism and the philosophy of the Sfas Emes have a particularly subtle approach to the issue of *humility* (see Pirke Avot 4:4, "Be exceedingly humble in spirit"). What should one do if one can't seem to be humble? Rabbi Stern writes:

> "Some individuals are unable to feel humble, despite their many efforts (they decline all honors, and yet feel possessed by a feeling of haughtiness and superiority). Rather than becoming depressed and frustrated [over one's lack of humility] which, after all, is itself a subtle form of haughtiness (how could someone as distinguished as myself lack the *middah* of humility?), the mishnah is encouraging us to accept with humility and grace our inability to attain this prized virtue." (Stern, 1999, p. 249)

Compare this attitude with that of Cohen, writing from the philosopher-therapist's point of view:

> "The most rational and rewarding form of self-assessment [avoids] two extremes: vanity and mock modesty. The vain person claims greater achievements than he has actually attained. The mock-modest person disclaims his achievements or belittles them...self-

damnation is an extreme form of mock modesty. It is a false, over-generalized, unrealistic *under*assessment of self-worth." (Cohen, 2007. p. 78)

At the same time, as Rabbi Stern notes, "excess spiritual satisfaction may breed a sense of smugness that may stifle one's growth" (Stern, 1999, p. 266).

Both Chassidic Judaism and REBT/CBT generally take the view that self-acceptance must be founded on a realistic and accurate assessment of one's virtues and vices, successes and failures—and that one does not condemn "the whole person," but rather, his or her inappropriate *behaviors.* Furthermore, both traditions emphasize the value of learning from one's mistakes—and even, of making mistakes! Thus, Cohen writes:

"Getting burned every so often by putting your hand in the proverbial fires of life can be a great teacher. You perform poorly on a job interview and use your experience to correct your mistakes on the next interview." (Cohen, 2007, p. 82)

Compare Cohen's point with the Talmudic concept of "loving reproof," as propounded in Pirke Avot 6.6, and the Chassidic understanding of this concept. Stern tells us, for example, "The Sfas Emes loved admonishment—and those who gave it" (Stern, 1999, p. 469). Indeed, the Chassidic view is that "the individual who is giving the admonishment is a true friend" and that "by lovingly accepting the criticisms of others, which motivates us to repent...we will merit Divine forgiveness" (Stern, 1999, pp. 468-9).

The Chassid (pious individual) "refuses to act unjustly to himself" (Stern, 1999, p. 427), either by bemoaning his failings or gloating over his successes. To put the idea in Cohen's more modern parlance, "Screw up gracefully. Accept yourself and learn from your mistakes" (Cohen, 2007, p. 82).

*****

We have already discussed the issue of "anger," in connection with CBT and REBT [see, e.g., "you can eliminate most of your despair or anger by changing your thinking or your self-talk." (Ellis & Harper, 1961, p. 186).]. We have also discussed Maimonides and his strong injunctions against anger. The Chassidic view of anger—not surprisingly—is also one of disapproval, though it allows for circumstances in which anger may be "justified." Even in such circumstances, however, the true *chassid* is "easily appeased" (Stern, 1999, p. 370; cf. Pirke Avot 5:14 re: "four types of temperament"). What is more surprising is the strikingly "REBT-oriented" attitude taken by Chassidic rabbis toward the *nature and genesis* of anger. Thus, Stern points out that anger produces harm "which one *inflicts upon oneself*" (p. 371) and:

> "There is nothing more foolish and short sighted than becoming angry and remaining in such an emotional state. It is the antithesis of *Yiddishkeit* and is described by *Chazal* [Talmudic sages] as tantamount to idolatry." (Stern, 1999, p. 371)

There are two principles articulated in the Chassidic position: first, that anger and its effects upon us are *self-inflicted*; and second, that there is a strong element of *narcissism* inherent in anger. This, in my view, is the meaning of the comparison between anger and idolatry: when we are angry, we kneel at the shrine of our own inflated ego. Rabbi and psychiatrist Abraham J. Twerski MD recounts a telling anecdote in this regard, concerning the Chassidic master, The Tzemach Tzedek:

> "When [he] felt he was being provoked to anger, he would study the laws pertaining to the prohibition of idol worship. He reasoned that inasmuch as the Talmud equates rage with idolatry, he needed to shore up his knowledge of this grievous sin, lest his anger [progress] to rage." (Twerski, 1995, pp. 172-73)

This thesis regarding anger is almost perfectly reflected in Ellis's CBT:

> "Feelings of anger are invariably reflections of one's own grandiosity. One essentially says, by feeling angry, (a) I do not like Joe's behavior and (b) because I do not like it, he *shouldn't* have acted that way. The second sentence here is actually a grandiose non sequitur...I am being unrealistic and god-like when I believe that my (or anyone else's) preference regarding Joe's behavior *should* make Joe act differently from the way he has acted." (Ellis and Harper, 1961, p. 104)

Rabbi Dr. Twerski also points out the foolishness of some fashionable "new age" ideas, concerning the expression of anger:

> "Some misguided psychologists advocate discharging one's anger by shouting or punching things. This is

utter nonsense, and serves only to intensify the anger...
the Chassidic master, the *Sfas Emes*, was accompanied
to the train-station by many of his followers. Before
boarding the train, he said to them, 'Do you know why
this single engine can pull so many heavy wagons? It
is because it contains the steam within itself." The
control of anger can be a powerful constructive force."
(Twerski, 1995, p. 173)

CHAPTER 6: THE MUSAR
MOVEMENT AND ITS CONTEMPORARIES

Rabbi Yaakov Menken (2005) defines Mussar (sometimes spelled *musar*) as "the study of ethics," but quickly adds:

> "It is so much more than that. It demands a personal commitment to moral values and to improving your behavior to meet that commitment. The goal of Mussar is to effect a self-transformation, by helping you to focus upon the type of person you want to be and the things standing in your way as you try to get there. Mussar is not about self-denial, but rather, about something considerably more difficult: self-control." (Menken, 2005, p. 157)

Arguably, the Mussar movement had its roots in the work of ibn Pakudahh of Saragosa, Spain, in the 11th century. We briefly discussed ibn Pakudahh earlier (p. 69), as a "forerunner of Maimonidean rationalism." But ibn Pakudahh's ethical treatise, "Duties of the Heart" (*Chovos HaLevavos*) is very much a precursor of the Mussar movement, which emerged some eight centuries later (Menken, 2005, p. 159).

Similarly, about a century before the formal Mussar movement began, Rabbi Moshe Chaim Luzzato (1707- 1747), in his magnum opus, *Mesilat Yesharim* (*Path of the Just*) took what Rabbi Menken calls,

> "A step by step approach to self-improvement, looking at good character traits…[and] explaining how to acquire each one; and also what pitfalls might prevent you from acquiring it." (Menken, 2005, p. 159)

We shall say much more about Rabbi Luzzato shortly. But perhaps the figure most associated with the Mussar movement is Reb Yisrael Salanter (Yisrael Lipkin, 1810-1883), who exerted great effort in disseminating Mussar works and setting up special "Mussar houses" for the teaching of Mussar (Menken, 2005, p. 159). According to Borowitz and Schwartz, the Mussar movement founded by Reb Yisrael "linked modern psychological insight to classic Jewish teaching about human nature" (Borowitz & Schwartz, 1999, p. 178). We will explore presently the specific ways in which Rabbi Salanter's methods and philosophy are closely aligned with those of CBT and REBT.

Rabbi Moshe Chaim Luzzato (1707- 1747)

Rabbi Moshe Chaim Luzzato—known as Ramchal—led a life that Rabbi Abraham Twerski describes as "brief, unbelievably productive, and terribly tragic." (Twerski, 1995, xii) Indeed, Ramchal died in an epidemic, just short of his fortieth birthday, having been thwarted from fulfilling his real passion—expounding on *Kabbalah* in *Eretz Yisrael* (the land of Israel). Notwithstanding Ramchal's passion for *Kabbalah*, his teachings on the emotions are closely linked with modern-day principles of CBT and REBT. For example, Ramchal writes of the need for one to become "master over himself" (Twersky, 1995, p. 56), and argues:

> "A furious person could destroy the whole world if he were able, because his intellect is not ruling over him at all, and he actually loses his rationality and becomes like all carnivorous beasts." (Heller and Rigler, 2005, p. 79)

Ramchal also shares with REBT the concept of "appropriate" versus "irrational" fear, and the need for "sound judgment" to distinguish the two (Twerski, 1995, p. 125). Ramchal cites several examples; i.e., "One may have an unrealistic fear of the cold, the heat, accidents, disease, the wind, etc." (Twerski, 1995, p. 124). Modern psychologists would probably view these as examples of "phobias," such as fear of heights, fear of closed spaces, etc. But Ramchal, citing Solomon [see Proverbs 26:13 re: "How could I go out? There is a lion out there in the road."] suggests that sometimes, anxiety is (in Rabbi Twerski's words) "a kind of rationalization, or an adaptation to justify a person's indolence" (Twerski, 1995, p. 124).

Although modern cognitive-behavioral psychologists would not assent to this etiology in most cases of phobic disorders—in which various forms of aversive "conditioning" are thought to play an important role—some types of avoidant behavior can *persist* because the individual finds it easier to *avoid the feared situation* than to confront it. And, to the extent that one also refuses to confront the *underlying irrational ideas* that are generating the anxiety, it could be argued that one is indeed indulging a kind of "indolence."

Ellis and Harper propose a similar mechanism for the maintenance of anxious avoidant behaviors, also citing a link between "indolence" and anxiety:

> "People who lead a lazy, passive existence and who keep saying that "nothing really interests me very much" are almost always (consciously or unconsciously) defending themselves against some irrational fear, especially the great fear of failure. Viewing failure with horror, they avoid certain activities that they would really like to engage in; and after sufficient avoidance, they conclude, in all sincerity, that they are not interested in these activities." (Ellis & Harper, 1961, p. 174)

*****

Ramchal's views resonate with the principles of REBT and CBT in several other important respects; e.g., Ramchal points out:

- The pitfalls of "allowing behavior to be dictated by habit" (Twerski, 1995, pp. 71-72)
- The risk that a "lack of diligence in learning" may lead to "faulty thinking" (Twerski, 1995, p. 110)
- The power of behavior to change one's inner states (Twerski, 1995, p. 117 and p. 181—cf. Ellis p. 185)

- The need to counteract feelings of dejection and regret by means of "sober thinking" and limiting one's needs (Twerski, 1995, pp. 255-56)
- The folly inherent in envy of others (Twerski, 1995, p. 173)

Let us examine each of these commonalities in more detail.

First, regarding the dangers of allowing oneself to be guided by habit rather than by careful reflection and analysis, Twerski observes:

"Ramchal emphasizes the danger in allowing behavior to be dictated by habit…[rather] every intelligent person should want his behavior to be determined by his intellect. If someone functions by habit, then he has essentially relinquished intellectual control of behavior." (Twerski, 1995, p. 71)

Ramchal begins by noting how the prophet Jeremiah berated the Israelites of his generation for being "oblivious to their actions," and "operating under the impetus of habit" (Twerski, 1995, p. 72). Ramchal attributes this tendency to "the *yetzer hara* [evil impulse]" which exerts "constant pressure on people so that they do not have adequate time to analyze which way they are going." (Twerski, 1995, p. 72)

Ellis and Harper speak similarly of this reflexive acquiescence to "habit"—usually, a "bad" habit or mode of thinking:

"Emotion in some major respects seems to be a kind of semi-logical, fixated, prejudiced, or bigoted thought, while thinking seems to be a relatively calm, unbiased, reflective kind of discrimination." (Ellis and Harper, 1961, p. 24)

Moreover:

"By the time a person…reaches adulthood, he has normally been conditioned to do almost all, if not absolutely all, his thinking, and consequently his emoting, in terms of self-talk or internalized phrases and sentences." (Ellis and Harper, 1961, p. 26)

Similarly, invoking Aristotle, cognitive therapist Elliott Cohen writes:

"Aristotle would…remind you that you become the sort of person you are by repeatedly doing the same things. You create your own irrational inclinations by continually acting irrationally. If you make a habit out of overeating, your stomach will accommodate more food, and you will find it…increasingly more difficult to eat in moderation. If you repeatedly retreat from social contexts, you will make yourself reclusive, and it will become increasingly more difficult to control yourself." (Cohen, 2007. p. 125)

In this regard, Rabbi Twerski writes of Ramchal:

"The Talmud states that if a person has committed a forbidden act twice, by the third time, he gives it no thought, and assumes it to be permissible (Yoma 86b).

This is the kind of danger Ramchal ascribes to habit."
(Twerski, 1995, p. 71)

*****

Citing a passage from Proverbs (24:30), Ramchal alludes to "the vineyard of a foolish person…overgrown with thorns, covered with weeds" and uses this as a metaphor for the dangers of indolence (Twerski, 1995, p. 110). Ramchal suggests that "the harmful consequences of indolence may not appear suddenly, but develop gradually…Lack of diligence in learning leads to deficiency in knowledge and then to faulty thinking." (Twerski, 1995, p. 110). The putative pathway, then, is essentially as follows:

Laziness → ignorance → faulty thinking

This pathway is quite similar to that cited by cognitive-behavioral therapists, as they seek to account for "faulty thinking" and its resultant discordant emotions. Ellis, in describing a particularly resistant and difficult patient, says to the woman, almost in desperation,

"If I could only get you to work at observing and changing your own self-defeating internal sentences, you'd be surprised how quickly and drastically your enormous feelings of anger…would go away… [but] you make little actual effort to grasp it: to see what your own sentences are and to examine the philosophic premises behind them." (Ellis and Harper, 1961, p. 31)

Ellis's implication is clear: if one is too "lazy" to challenge one's deeply-held but irrational beliefs, one will indulge in faulty thinking that leads to emotional distress.

Similarly, Cohen points to the hazards of "laxness" in assessing evidence, and clearly supports Ramchal's conviction regarding "the harmful consequences of indolence:"

> "Ignorance is often at the root of underconfidence and overconfidence in managing risks…For example, I know of one fellow who boasted how he drank from his friend's cup with full knowledge that [his friend] had the flu. This poor fellow ended up almost dying from the flu. It is such laxness and overconfidence in the management of health risks that can lead to widespread epidemics." (Cohen, 2007, p. 245)

*****

As the reader well knows by now, one of the cardinal principles of CBT/REBT is that actively changing one's behavior—e.g., from maladaptive to adaptive—can lead to profound changes in the way one *feels*, emotionally. Such concerted action may also fundamentally alter the way one "is;" that is, one's *character* may be shaped by one's behavior, rather than (or in addition to) the other way around. As Twerski notes "Just as a fervent desire leads to *Zerizus* [roughly, *devotion*], the reverse can also be true: *Zerizus* can lead to fervor" (Twerski. 1995, p. 117).

Ramchal clearly endorses this view of human emotion, as we see in several key teachings. Thus, he tells us:

"It is known that what is most desirable in the Divine service is the devotion of the heart…[but] if one lacks this fervor, it is advisable that he act by force of will, because *outer movements awaken inner ones*." (Twerski 1995, p. 117, italics added)

Rabbi Twerski—a psychiatrist, let us recall—expounds on this idea:

"The Talmud states that a person should engage in *mitzvos* [commandments] even if he does not have the proper *kavannah* (intent and concentration) because the *kavannah* will come with the action (Pesachim 50b)…if you do not have the enthusiasm for mitzvos, do them anyway with diligence and the enthusiasm will follow…[Similarly] the traditional psychotherapeutic approach…was that symptoms were the result of deep-rooted emotional traumas and unresolved conflicts. The theory was that a thorough understanding of these [traumas and conflicts] would eliminate the symptoms. Repeated treatment failures led to this psychodynamic approach being increasingly replaced by a behavioristic approach; namely, change behavior first, and the internal problems can then be resolved. Working from the outside in has proven to be much more effective than working from the inside out." (Twerski 1995, pp. 117-118)

While not all psychotherapists (and probably few psychoanalysts!) would give such whole-hearted support to the cognitive-behavioral model, Rabbi Twerski has stated the essence of the approach taken in CBT and REBT. Thus, in describing how one can conquer phobic anxiety re: riding on buses, Ellis and Harper tell us:

> "You must force yourself, over and over again, to keep riding on busses and to keep telling yourself, while riding, rational counter-propaganda to eradicate your irrational self-sentences. The more you do the things you are afraid of…the quicker and more thoroughly your needless anxieties will vanish." (Ellis & Harper, 1961, p. 141)

The critical importance of simple and repeated practice is also stressed by Ramchal when he discusses the mitzvah of *Nekiyus* (roughly, *being free of a predisposition to sin*—see Twerski, 1995, p. 128). Ramchal writes:

> "There is no denying that achievement of *Nekiyus* may call for some effort…[but] if one sets one's mind to achieve this admirable trait, just a bit of practice will make it much easier than one thinks it is." (Twerski, 1995, pp. 180-81)

Indeed, citing Rabbi Elimelech of Lizensk (1717-87), Twerski notes that "…many habits can be overcome simply by making an effort to do otherwise for thirty consecutive days. It is often a question of overcoming inertia" (Twerski, 1995, p. 181).

*****

As we have seen several times in our discussion of Chassidic *rebbeim* (rabbis), the struggle against depression or dejection was often a paramount concern (e.g., see Nahman of Bratslav and Arthur Green's description of Nahman's depression). Indeed, as Twerski notes:

> "The Chassidic master of Karlin said, 'Whereas there is no explicit Torah commandment prohibiting dejection, it can cause a person to commit the most serious transgressions.'" (Twerski, 1995, p. 256)

For Ramchal, too, overcoming dejection and regret is an important spiritual goal. In order to do this, we must *overcome obstacles* and *strive to attain joy (simcha)*. Thus, Ramchal tells us that for spiritually-realized beings (those who have reached the level of *Chassidus*):

> "The more obstacles placed in their path, the more courage and strength they muster to overcome them." (Twerski, 1995, p. 251)

Those of this high spiritual level of development also cultivate joy:

> "*simchah* (joy)...is a fundamental principle in the Divine service...The Talmud says, 'The Divine presence comes to rest only where there is joy in doing mitzvos."(*Shabbos* 30b) (Twerski, 1995, p. 254)

Rabbi Israel Salanter

Rabbi Yisrael [Israel] Salanter (1810-83) is often considered the founder of the Mussar movement. But "Rabbi Yisrael" (as he is affectionately known) was much more than that. In his classic work, *Israel Salanter: Text, Structure, Idea* (1982), Hillel Goldberg describes Rabbi Salanter as follows:

> "An ethicist, early psychologist of the unconscious, Talmud scholar, reader of kabbalistic and Jewish philosophic literature; communal leader, bridge figure between East and West European Jewry, [and] troubled saint." (Goldberg, 1982, vii)

Our interest in Rabbi Salanter, of course, lies primarily in those ideas of his that resonate with the principles of CBT and REBT—and there are many. Indeed, much of Rabbi Salanter's program for moral and spiritual development rests on the foundation of *cognitive modification and re-structuring*. However, as Goldberg makes clear, this hoped-for transformation is something of a "long shot" for most human beings. This is because of the tremendous susceptibility of humankind to the urges of *yetzer hara*—the evil impulse. Thus:

> "He [Rabbi Salanter] cautioned his followers: 'A person's imagination leads him wildly in the direction of his heart's sinful desires, fearing not the inevitable future when God will hold him accountable for all his deeds.'" [from *Iggeret Hamusar*; in Borowitz & Schwartz, 1999, p. 178)

Indeed, Rabbi Salanter speaks of the "intellect's impotence" in the face of these powerful urges toward evil-doing (Goldberg, 1982, p. 27). And yet—with sufficient will, dedication, and practice in the ways of Mussar, man might "surmount his self-deception…his wracking passions, and the snares of death" (Goldberg, 1982, p. 27).

Thus, we learn that "the impotence of the intellect is not fixed…[it] can be galvanized" so as to transcend the forces of evil (Goldberg, 1982, p. 28), and to oppose what Rabbi Salanter calls *hush* [*chush*]. This is a complex term that is difficult to translate into English, but Goldberg suggests that *hush* is best translated as "sense-experience," including "both the visual and the instinctual" (Goldberg, 1982, pp. 29-30).

One might make a very rough comparison between *hush* and Freud's concept of the *id*—the primitive, instinctual part of the psyche that is kept under wraps by the ego and superego. In his book on Rabbi Salanter, Hillel Goldberg generally eschews the notion that Salanter is "a forerunner of Freud" (Goldberg, 1982, p. 10). He does note:

> "Rabbi Israel unequivocally reflects the sensitivity to irrationality that courses through the works of nineteenth-century Western European thinkers like Schopenhauer and later Nietzsche and Freud." (Goldberg, 1982, p. 151)

However, in his forward to Alan Moranis's book, *Jacob's Ladder*, Goldberg is more expansive on the connections between Rabbi Salanter and Freud:

"Keen psychological understanding gave Salanter's Mussar both its solidity and elusiveness. Writing in Hebrew, before Sigmund Freud, Salanter articulated a psychology of the unconscious and extracted from it implications for the religious quest. A person could never be certain of his motives, since he might not be conscious of them. To be sure that one's prayer, charity or interpersonal relationships were not soiled by unworthy desires for power or prestige (for example), one needed a system for self-analysis. Once unworthy motives were identified, one needed methods for changing oneself...Salanter's best students became both Talmudic scholars and adepts at analyzing human behavior—their own and that of others. All of his students learned to see the quest for God within the quest for integrity in human relationships, including one's relationship with oneself." (Goldberg, Mussar Institute)

*****

And so, what can the very vulnerable human being do to push back against *hush*? How exactly does one "change" oneself? As part of Mussar study, Rabbi Salanter advocates a process of "cognitive purification." Goldberg describes this as "a highly emotional mode of study." On the one hand, for Rabbi Salanter, cognitive purification entails mastery of "correct ideas"—an obvious affinity with REBT and CBT. On the other hand, this process is not one of dry, intellectual apprehension: the heart must also be engaged. In Salanter's words, learning must occur "with lips aflame" (Goldberg, 1982,

p. 33). In practice, this might involve "singing or chanting or weeping or humming or shouting as verbal accompaniment to sifting correct from incorrect ideas" so that the correct ideas "profoundly impress themselves upon the inner being." (Goldberg, 1982, p. 33)

This highly emotive context of learning reminds us of psychotherapist Frieda Fromm-Reichmann's dictum regarding psychotherapy: *the patient doesn't need an explanation, but an experience.* Psychotherapist David Wallin understands this to mean that "the patient needs a relationship more than a reason why" he or she has certain emotional problems (Wallin, 2007, p. 126). But we may also understand both Fromm-Reichmann and Rabbi Salanter as alluding to a kind of *transformative emotional context*, shaped by the often intense relationship with a therapist—or *rebbe*. This concept of the "corrective emotional experience" was elucidated in the 1940s by psychiatrists Franz Alexander and Thomas Morton French. They meant that the essential function of psychotherapy was:

> "...to re-expose the patient, under more favorable circumstances, to emotional situations which he could not handle in the past. The patient, in order to be helped, must undergo a *corrective emotional experience* suitable to repair the traumatic influence of previous experiences." (Alexander & French, 1946, p.66, italics added)

This is extraordinarily similar to Rabbi Salanter's program for self-change, though he might have substituted the phrase "undo the baneful influences of the evil impulse" for the phrase, "repair the traumatic influence of previous experiences." As Goldberg puts it, for Rabbi Salanter:

> "Ironically, intellect is rendered efficacious by [the] very stratum that it seeks to mold, the emotions. According to Rabbi Israel, a normative idea that is not merely understood but grasped in the cauldron of inflamed emotion becomes a galvanized idea which penetrates and drives the inner being and thereby catalyzes normative behavior." (Goldberg, 1982, pp. 34-35)

All this has been amply confirmed by modern neuropsychology, which has demonstrated that learning is more firmly established (consolidated) in the brain when there is an emotional "charge" to the learned material or the learning environment. In fact, in a paper aptly entitled, "Make mild moments memorable: add a little arousal," Dr. J.L. McGaugh notes that "emotionally arousing stimuli enhance long-term memory of immediately preceding neutral stimuli" (McGaugh, 2006, p. 345). Perhaps Rabbi Salanter reached this same conclusion more than a century earlier than modern neurobiologists.

So far, we have compared Rabbi Salanter's concept of "cognitive purification" to the "corrective emotional experience" described in the *psychoanalytic* literature. But how does Rabbi Salanter's form of learning relate to the main focus of our inquiry: REBT and CBT? We already alluded to the role of "correct ideas" in Rabbi Salanter's schema of Mussar instruction. The affinities with REBT and CBT in this *ideational* realm are clear. But what may be less obvious is that many cognitive therapists—consistent with Rabbi Salanter's musar program—recognize the strong "emotive" element in their work with patients. Ellis and Harper, for example, might not use the Salanterian expression "the cauldron of inflamed emotion" to describe the atmosphere in their office—but their published exchanges with patients show clearly that these clinicians appreciated the importance of *intense emotion* in bringing about therapeutic change. For example, Dr. Robert A. Harper here recounts his interaction with a patient he calls "Marlo," a 23-year-old woman who believed that "all men were no good" and who presented in therapy with suicidal ideation related to two recent "break-ups:"

> M: "I know it's my privilege to take my life. And since I find that it's just not worth going on with it, that's exactly what I intend to do. It's a phony deal. No one can be trusted or depended upon. Things always end up the same."

> RH: "How so? Just because two lovers in a row have left you? That's a hell of a big conclusion from a pitifully small bit of evidence!"

> M: "Just the same—it's always the same."

> RH: "Hogwash! How can a bright girl like you believe such twaddle?"

(Ellis and Harper, 1961, p. 56)

Similarly, Albert Ellis was renowned for his use of salty language and barnyard expletives, in forcefully confronting the irrational ideas of his patients. Following Ellis's death in 2007, a posting on the website of the American Psychological Association noted:

> "Known as "the Lenny Bruce of psychotherapy," [Ellis] was widely known for his zinging one-liners on people's follies: "All humans are out of their f—-ing minds, every single one of them," he liked to say." (DeAngelis, 2007)

In part, this attitude may have reflected Ellis's "no-nonsense" approach to life in general. But, in this psychiatrist's opinion, both Ellis and Harper understood the importance of, metaphorically speaking, raising the temperature in the therapeutic milieu—creating, if not a Salanterian "cauldron," at least a kind of salutary hot-house.

*****

We have pointed out many times that *self-examination* is a foundational element of REBT and CBT; in particular, the necessity of scrutinizing one's irrational or destructive beliefs. In our section on "the imperative of self-awareness and self-examination," we cited two passages relevant to REBT and CBT. Ellis and Harper commented on our basic, human tendency:

> "To devise superficially rational or seemingly plausible explanations or excuses for one's acts, beliefs, or desires,

usually without being aware that these are not one's real motives. Psychologically, therefore, rationalizing or excusing one's behavior is virtually the opposite of being rational about it." (Ellis & Harper, 1961, p. 67)

And Rabbi Dr. Twerski observed:

"People of greater intelligence are more likely to be more expert at rationalizations. Any psychotherapist will testify that the most sophisticated patients are apt to be the most difficult to treat, because they believe most strongly in their own lies." (Twerski, 1995, p. 112)

Now, Rabbi Salanter is also keenly aware both of the need for "examination of the self" (Goldberg, 1982, p. 37) and of our tendency *to deceive ourselves*. Goldberg, for example, quotes Rabbi Salanter as saying that "Most of the time, people view themselves mistakenly…they recognize neither their deficiencies nor their unworthy character traits." (Goldberg, 1982, p. 37, from *Homiletical Discourses* D8:15, p.38). To counteract this, Rabbi Salanter counsels self-examination while "putting truth in the mind's eye" (Goldberg, 1982, p. 37); i.e., comparing one's actual traits with the ideal. But given our tendency toward self-deception, the individual alone may not be able to assess this ratio accurately. Rabbi Salanter therefore recommends Mussar study:

"In conjunction with others…[such that] the hazards of self-deception can be materially reduced when an intimate friend points out one's unworthy deeds and character traits." (Goldberg, 1982, p. 3)

In fact, Rabbi Salanter also urges "indirect group musar study" so that "the participants will strengthen each other, diminish the foolishness of each other's hearts, and dissolve each other's laziness." It is essential, however, that this kind of corrective feedback be provided in a manner that will "let everyone guard the dignity of his fellow" (Goldberg, 1982, p. 37). This approach has striking affinities with CBT or REBT carried out in a group setting. Psychologist John R. White describes the rationale for cognitive-behavioral group therapy (CBGT) by means of this example:

> "A client can test a hypothesis by deliberately setting up a situation to determine whether the hypothesis is proved to be valid. For example, a shy client believed that if he opened up, he would be ignored by the people around him. With the support of the other clients, he decided to test that hypothesis in group by speaking up and assessing the reactions he received. Contrary to his expectation, he found that people were interested in what he had to say and demonstrated their warmth and concern." (White & Freeman, 2000, p. 6)

In summary, Rabbi Salanter's emphasis on self-examination; the detection of rationalization; and the use of group "feedback" to correct both irrational beliefs and self-deception have strong affinities with the techniques of CBT and REBT.

*****

Both CBT and REBT emphasize that self-transformation requires more than simply acquiring rational ideas: *one must put the ideas into practice.* This is very forcefully expressed in Rabbi Salanter's program of Mussar study as well. Thus, Goldberg observes that for Rabbi Salanter:

> "Intellect can be purified. Through arduous, persistent labor at musar study, both in groups and in solitude; and through unflinching self-scrutiny…intellect gradually sheds the bonds of raw passion." (Goldberg, 1982, p. 53)

But, as Goldberg insists, Rabbi Salanter's ideas "can be understood fully *only by implementing them.* To him, it was less important that his thought be grasped systematically, as a whole, than that each segment of his thought be absorbed fully…[so that] their latent interrelationships would emerge *in their execution*" (Goldberg, 1982, p. 55, italics added).

Furthermore, in theory:

> "Behavioral alteration and intellectual endeavor are disjunct, in practice, success at intellectual endeavor is far more likely with prior success at behavioral alteration. The behavioral and the intellectual processes are correlative, distinct but not disjunct." (Goldberg, 1982, p. 117)

For Rabbi Salanter, transformation of the self requires "repeated efforts at self-restraint." Such practice "slows the speed at which aroused, unworthy soul forces are manifested in behavior…[and] the more one observes commandments precisely as they are defined in *halakha*, the more one weakens one's inclinations that run counter to normative action… *provided that the normative act is performed repeatedly.*" (Goldberg, 1982, p. 141, emphasis added). Indeed, for Rabbi Salanter, "Reason alone cannot make [one] subjugate his urges to sin; it is necessary to engage in habitual self-restraint" (Goldberg, 1982, p. 143).

Rabbi Salanter's ideas are integrally related to the theories that underlie CBT, REBT, and a variant of REBT called "Logic Based Therapy" (LBT), developed by Dr. Elliott Cohen. Cohen explains how, for example, changes in one's ideas are reinforced by changes in one's *behavior:*

> "According to LBT, when people counter irrational… [ideas] with rational antidotal reasoning, a state of cognitive dissonance arises. This is a state where a client intellectually perceives the irrationality of her syllogism but is still inclined to deduce its destructive conclusion. For example, despite the fact that John may now see that he shouldn't succumb to his blind passion to steal the BMW by making…excuses for himself, he may still be inclined to steal the car. In overcoming the inertia of cognitive dissonance… LBT stresses the cultivation of willpower. Following philosopher Aristotelis Santas, it construes willpower as a muscle that can be strengthened by repeatedly flexing it. Just as a body builder cannot bench press large amounts without building up to it, *people can develop their willpower muscle through incremental practice.* Behavioral assignments can be made to help

strengthen willpower. Accordingly, LBT prescribes homework assignments in which clients are asked to practice ("flex") their willpower muscles...For example, a client who is working on anger control could work on not yelling at the ticket-taker at the toll booth (say, for moving too slowly) before working up to more challenging feats such as not yelling at his aggressive teenage son." (Cohen, 2006)

In this same vein, we close with a passage we examined earlier (Chapter 1), from Ellis and Harper:

"Don't just think: *act*! Years or decades of past fright and inertia may almost always be overcome by days or weeks of present forced practice...thinking and doing; these are the unmagical keys that will unlock almost any chest of past defeats and turn them into possible present and future victories." (Ellis and Harper, 1961, p. 162)

*****

Cognitive-behavioral therapists often speak of irrational ideas as *habitual modes of thinking not based on careful empirical observation*. Thus, Cohen writes:

"Two of the most common ways in which people tend to oversimplify reality are by *pigeonholing* and *stereotyping*. Both of these forms of judgment oversimplify reality by failing to discern significant aspects of it. They underlie a host of traits of character that impede human flourishing, including narrow-mindedness, intolerance, inflexibility, prejudice... [and] bigotry." (Cohen, 2007, p. 206)

Similarly, for Rabbi Salanter, we must confront and free ourselves from what he calls "soul-forces," which are defined as "deep-seated biases" (Goldberg, 1982, p. 118). These prejudicial soul-forces "generate unworthy behavior in the absence of dispassionate guidance by man" (Goldberg, 1982, p. 106).

But despite the exhortations of both Mussar and CBT, both Rabbi Salanter and cognitive-behavioral therapists understand the limitations of human rationality and self-transformation. We are not "logic machines," nor are we passionless demi-gods. As Ellis and Harper bluntly acknowledge:

"Yes, man is a highly reasonable, brain-using animal. But he also has distinct biological tendencies to act in the most ridiculous, prejudiced, amazingly asinine ways. He is, quite normally and naturally, inclined to be childish, suggestible, superstitious, bigoted, and downright idiotic...he has such great difficulty achieving and sustaining a level of sound and sane behavior that he rarely does so for any length of time, but keeps instead continually falling back to his puerile ways." (Ellis and Harper, 1961, p. 52)

Rabbi Salanter says much the same thing, in somewhat more restrained language:

"Man, inasmuch as he is man, even though it is within his capacity and power to strip...his intellect from the arousal of his soul-forces…nonetheless man is human, his soul-forces are in him, [and] it is not within his power to separate them…from his intellect. Thus it is not within man's capacity to arrive at True Intellect… [wholly separated from soul-forces]." (from *Tevunah*; cited in Goldberg, 1982, p. 119)

In short, it is not within our power to be "rational" at all times and in all ways. We are fallible human beings who must constantly regain the lost ground of wisdom. Yet Rabbi Salanter is at least open to the possibility that mankind *might* make spiritual progress—in effect, becoming on the inside what had been evident only externally:

"With the right intellectual and behavioral training, [man's] mind and body will be successfully assimilated unto the commandments of specific deeds, and the commandments of character. The commandments which were external to him as he approached them will become part of him." (Goldberg, 1982, p. 144)

The Chofetz Chaim

Rabbi Yisrael Meir HaCohen Kagan (1838-1933), better known as the *Chofetz Chaim*, after his famous book of that title, made major contributions to Mussar. He is renowned for his voluminous writings on *lashon hara* (or *loshon hora*), roughly translated as "the evil tongue," which was the subject of his book, *Sefer Shmiras Haloshon*—literally, the "book of the guarding of the tongue" (Finkelman & Berkowitz, 1995, note to reader). But whereas the avoidance of harmful speech is the focus of the Chofetz Chaim's work. many principles in his teachings relate to more general behavioral concerns; e.g., to *self-discipline*; *the breaking of "bad habits;"* and *the need to "train" oneself in proper behavior.*

From the standpoint of the Chofetz Chaim, *lashon hara* represents what psychologists might consider a pathological form of *narcissism;* i.e., the deliberate use of derogatory speech represents:

> "The belief that everyone and everything should conform to one's own standard. It arises out of intolerance of differences between oneself and others… [*lashon hara* reflects] the sense that one's own way is the right way." (Finkelman & Berkowitz, 1995, p. xxxvi)

This framework has close affinities with that of REBT and the views of Ellis and Harper, Elliot Cohen, and others. For example, Ellis and Harper argue:

> "Feelings of anger are invariably reflections of one's own grandiosity. One essentially says, by feeling angry, (a) I do not like Joe's behavior; and (b) because I do not like it, he *shouldn't* have acted that way…[but] I am being unrealistic and god-like when I believe that *my* (or anyone else's) preference regarding Joe's behavior should make Joe act differently." (Ellis and Harper, 1961, p. 104)

For the Chofetz Chaim, we neutralize such narcissism by controlling our speech, which actually allows us to perceive the world through a different lens:

"*Shmiras HaLoshon* ["guarding of the tongue"] is the prism through which one can see the validity in the various paths and opinions among well-meaning people. Even without agreeing or seeing the value of someone else's way of thinking, one can accept it as valid." (Finkelman & Berkowitz, 1995, xxxvi)

Furthermore, for the Chofetz Chaim, as for the cognitive therapist, one's *feelings* are a consequence of one's habitual *behavior, perceptions and cognitions.* Thus:

"*Loshon hora* breeds unhappiness in the speaker... [who] *trains himself* in bitterness and complaining. In his eyes, he is surrounded by irritating, inconsiderate, flawed people who make his world a disappointing, uncomfortable place. He *makes it his habit* to look past the [godly] image of his fellow Jew and gaze intently at his every flaw. *His perceptions* fill his heart with anger and disdain." (Finkelman & Berkowitz, 1995, xxxvii, italics added)

In contrast, one who follows the laws of *Shmiras Haloshon* "trains oneself to focus on the good" (Finkelman & Berkowitz, 1995, xxxviii). And what is the path toward "guarding the tongue?" It lies in a concerted effort to break "bad habits." Thus:

"It is a proven fact that the longer one persists in guarding his tongue, the easier it becomes." (Finkelman & Berkowitz, 1995, p. 63)

Indeed:

> "In place of the illusory power conferred by becoming the source of gossip, the person who guards his speech builds real power. This is the power of self-discipline, the knowledge that one has control over his impulses, that he has the inner strength to restrain himself, measure his words, and act in accordance with the highest aspects of himself." (Finkelman & Berkowitz, 1995, p xxxviii)

Furthermore:

> "One should train himself like someone learning a craft, to exercise restraint in speech. One must reach the point where such restraint comes naturally to him." (Finkelman & Berkowitz, 1995, p. 219)

In addition, for the Chofetz Chaim, as for cognitive therapists, we have a responsibility to understand *why* we behave inappropriately:

> "When one is afflicted with a penchant for a particular form of negative behavior, he must determine its *root cause* and eradicate it." (Finkelman & Berkowitz, 1995, p. 307, italics added)

For the Cofetz Chaim, *anger* is an important root cause of *loshon hora*. Following the Zohar, the Chofetz Chaim conceives anger as a sort of "foreign god" before which the susceptible individual bows down; i.e., the one overcome by anger "*allows a* foreign god to dwell within himself" (Finkelman & Berkowitz, 1995, p. 311, italics added). Note that this teaching points to a degree of *complicity* or *volition*, in our yielding to anger. In contrast, the righteous individual "guards the sanctity of his soul and does not allow it to be uprooted and replaced by that 'foreign god' (anger)" (Finkelman & Berkowitz, 1995, p. 311). In essence, for the Cofetz Chaim, as for the cognitive therapist, we have a certain degree of control over our negative emotions. Thus, "it is imperative that one rid his heart of anger" (Finkelman & Berkowitz, 1995, p. 311).

This is not to say that the fallible human being will never slip back into the old, injurious ways of anger and *loshon hora*, from time to time. But like cognitive therapists, the Chofetz Chaim counsels persistence, patience, and self-acceptance:

> "One should not grow frustrated if, after he resolved to avoid forbidden speech, his evil inclination got the better of him and he spoke *loshon hora*. Even if this happens time and again, nevertheless, he should not despair. Rather, he should forever strengthen himself to avoid improper speech, and persevere." (Finkelman & Berkowitz, 1995, p. 63)

Similarly, therapist and philosopher Elliot Cohen asks:

> "But what if you act and fail, falling flat on your face? Does that not lessen your self-worth?...No. Failing is an essential part of trying. And if you don't try, you damn well won't succeed...getting burned every so often by putting your hand in the proverbial fires of life can be a great teacher." (Cohen, 2007, p. 81)

The Chofetz Chaim understands that sometimes, in the context of a loving relationship, it is permissible to listen to *loshon hora*—at least, up to a point, and with certain caveats. Thus, Rabbis Finkelman and Berkowitz note:

> "When a husband or wife is in need of emotional support in dealing with difficulty…listening [to lashon hara] under such circumstances is constructive and is clearly permissible." (Finkelman & Berkowitz, 1995, p. 254)

Nevertheless, the Chofetz Chaim would hold:

> "When possible, one should attempt to help one's spouse *understand the situation* in a way that would relieve his or her anger or frustration. If one finds that his or her spouse is forever in need of "letting off steam," it is important to try to bring about a general *change of attitude* through discussion, reading or audio material, or suggesting a meeting with a rabbi or other qualified individual." (Finkelman & Berkowitz, 1995, p. 254, italics added)

Indeed, for the Chofetz Chaim, as for the cognitive therapists, *understanding and investigation* are critical tools in the construction of one's character and behavior. As Rabbis Finkelman and Berkowitz note:

> "Even when one has personally witnessed a situation, he must avoid hastily concluding that one party…[is at fault]. Generally speaking, it is impossible to fully

understand the attitude and behavior of one person towards another without a thorough knowledge of their relationship until this point. What may appear as one person's plotting against the other may, in reality, be an act of self-defense." (Finkelman & Berkowitz, 1995, p. 330)

Similarly, therapist Elliot Cohen admonishes us:

"Instead of believing on insufficient evidence, question all that you believe...cast off your stereotypes and believe only that for which you can muster adequate evidence." (Cohen, 2007, pp. 224-25)

*****

As Rabbis Finkelman and Berkowitz point out, the teachings of the Chofetz Chaim require:

"In striving to develop the quality of *shmiras haloshon*, one must place great emphasis on reacting toward any situation with *savlanus*; that is to be tolerant of whatever negativity is thrown one's way...a savlan is capable of hearing insult in silence. He *tells himself* that whatever occurs is an expression of Divine will, and that in reality, his own sins are the true causes of his being shamed." (Finkelman & Berkowitz, 1995, p. 273, italics added)

This passage is striking in a number of respects relevant to CBT and REBT. In the broadest sense, both the concept of *savlanus* and the goals of REBT/CBT have strong affinities with the ancient Stoic idea of *apatheia* –which we may understand not as our modern-day "apathy" but as something like "equanimity" or "peace of mind" (Pies, 2008, p. x). Historically, it is likely that the rabbis of the Talmud were strongly influenced by Stoic teachings current at the time of the Roman Emperor, Marcus Aurelius (121-180 CE), and it is plausible that these Stoic "threads" in Talmudic Judaism extended in attenuated form to the time of the Chofetz Chaim. Similarly, Albert Ellis has explicitly invoked the teachings of the Stoic philosopher, Epictetus (ca. 55-135AD), and those of Marcus Aurelius, as progenitors of REBT (Ellis & Harper, 1961, p. 5).

Even more striking, however, is the idea expressed in the above passage that what the individual tells himself has a direct impact on *how and what he perceives and feels*. To be sure, Ellis would not endorse the notion that "whatever occurs is an expression of Divine will, and that in reality, [one's] own sins are the true causes of his being shamed." But an underlying principle is shared by both the Chofetz Chaim and cognitive therapists; namely, that the way we feel is a consequence of *what we tell ourselves*. Indeed, therapist Elliot Cohen paraphrases Epictetus as follows: "When you are disturbed, don't blame others; blame your own irrational inferences" (Cohen, 2007, p.116).

CHAPTER 7:
MODERN RABBINICAL VIEWS

To some degree, this last chapter heading is one of arbitrary convenience. After all, the Chofetz Chaim's birth and death dates (1838-1933) overlap considerably with those of Rabbi Abraham Isaac Kook (1865-1935), yet we dealt with the Chofetz Chaim in the section on Mussar. To some extent, we can point to "modernist" trends in the work of some rabbis considered in this section—depending on how we choose to define "modern"—but this designation, too, seems rather arbitrary. Rabbi Kook, for example, was certainly caught up in "modern" issues, such as the rancorous debates over the establishment of the State of Israel. Yet in many ways, the writings and orientation of Rabbi Kook remind one of the mystics and seers of centuries past, such as Rabbi Judah Loew of Prague and other Cabbalists (Bokser, 1978). So, too, with Rabbi Kalonymus Kalman Shapira (1889–1943), who perished in the Holocaust. Although Rabbi Shapira's journal makes reference to some aspects of modernity—e.g., his strikingly negative comments about "today's secular psychologists"(Shapira, 1995, p. 152)—much of his journal could have been written two centuries earlier, by any of the great Chassidic *rebbeim* of Europe. In partial contrast, the writings of Rebbe Menachem Mendel Schneerson (1902-1994) often have an overtly "modern" ring to them, as when the Rebbe discusses computers and artificial hearts (Jacobson, 1995, p. 270). Of course, the Rebbe lived well into the late 20th century—in that sense, the most "modern" of sages discussed in this section.

Rabbi Abraham Isaak Kook (1865-1935)

Rabbi Abraham Isaak Kook—also known by the honorific, "Rav Kook"—is so protean a figure that any biographical synopsis runs the risk of oversimplifying. Perhaps a fair summary is provided by one of Rabbi Kook's most respected interpreters, Rabbi Jacob Agus:

> "Rav Kook was a mystic, a philosopher and a saint. He was a preeminent Talmudic scholar…[and also] a Lurianic Kabbalist, engaged in cultivating the various grades of mystical ecstasy…However, his main concern was not the salvation of individuals, but the redemption of the Jewish people and of all mankind." (from Preface I, in Bokser, 1978, xi)

Rabbi Kook was an almost exact contemporary of Sigmund Freud (1856-1939). At first glance, these two great Jewish figures would seem to have very little in common. Crudely (and somewhat inaccurately) stated, one might contrast Kook "the mystic" with Freud "the rationalist" and assume that there would be little or no common ground between them. And yet, Rabbi Bezalel Naor was struck by one similarity:

> "Rav Kook put little, if any, stock in the veneer of respectability with which Europe cloaks itself. Beneath the surface there is ample latitude for immorality. Though to the best of my knowledge, Rav Kook never mentions him by name, nor does he allude to his theories, one is reminded at this point of the discoveries of the Viennese psychiatrist, Sigmund Freud." (Naor, 1998)

Naor points out in a footnote that, "Rav Kook's son, Zevi Yehuda Kook (1891-1992), does on one occasion refer (negatively) to the "theory of the unconscious." Yet it seems that Rabbi Kook himself—like Freud—was able to see beneath the surface of the human psyche, into the darker currents that run through man and society.

Whatever Rav Kook would have made of psychoanalytic theory, I believe that he would have been in sympathy with a number of principles found in CBT and REBT. To begin with, Rabbi Kook recognizes that *the individual must be true to his or her unique nature*, and not be overly-concerned with the opinions of others. And, notwithstanding his overriding interest in the "redemption of the Jewish people and of all mankind," Rabbi Kook recognized that *transforming oneself* can lead to changes in the wider world:

> "I must find my happiness within my inner self, *unconcerned whether people agree with me*, or by what is happening to my own career. The more I shall recognize my own identity, and the more I will

permit myself to be original, and to stand on my own feet…the more will the light of God shine on me, and the more will my potentialities develop to serve as a blessing to myself *and to the world.* The refinements to which I subject myself, my thoughts, my imagination, my morals, and my emotions, *will also serve as general refinements for the whole world.*" (from *Arple Tohar*, p. 22, cited in Bokser, 1978, p. 30, italics added)

Compare the foregoing passage with this one, from Ellis and Harper:

"If you could, theoretically, always win the approval of those whose love you "need," you would have to spend so much time and energy doing so that you would have little time left for other pursuits. Striving ceaselessly to be approved means living your life for what others think and want you to do, rather than for your own goals…[as well as] selling your own soul and losing your self-respect… Ironically enough, the greater your need for being loved, *the less people will tend to respect and care for you.*" (Ellis & Harper, 1961, p. 84, italics added)

Indeed, for Rabbi Kook, there is a direct parallel between one's willingness to *change oneself* for the better, and one's ability to *change society* for the better. He writes:

"In truth, one cannot rise to the spiritual level of seeking the reformation of society without a deep inner repentance of every sin and wrongdoing." (from

The Lights of Penitence, quoted in Bokser, 1978, p. 50)

This is entirely consonant with Mussar teachings, as Alan Morinis observes:

"The task is to fill yourself up with wisdom and knowledge until you brim over, and the overflow spills out of you and into the adjacent vessels, who are other people." (Morinis, 2007, p. 16)

For Rabbi Kook, as for the cognitive therapists, one's inner transformation cannot come about *unless we begin to change entrenched, self-defeating habits.* And perhaps then, society, too, may change. Thus, in an essay entitled, "The Pangs of Cleansing," Rabbi Kook writes:

"As long as a person orders his life on the basis of a fixed pattern, he will not be able to escape his intellectual, moral and practical deficiencies, and how will he be able to mend himself? *We must therefore not permit habit to be the primary factor in our social or personal life.* The individual person as well as society at large must always seek to correct itself and to mend its spiritual and practical defects." (Bokser, 1978, p. 266, italics added)

In short—to cite an aphorism usually attributed to the Maharishi Mahesh Yogi!—"For the forest to be green, each tree must be green."

*****

It clearly would be a mistake to cast Rabbi Kook in the role of a "rationalist" philosopher, in the mode, say, of a Spinoza or a Maimonides. As Rabbi Kook tells us in his essay, "The Road to Renewal:"

"The nature of the spiritual reality cannot be discerned through scientific probing. Objective knowledge, rational analysis, philosophy—these disclose only the external phenomena of life…the true achievement of rational demonstration is only to prepare a path for the spirit to reach the outer chamber of the spiritual domain." (Bokser, 1978, p. 287)

And yet, despite his mystical "core," Rabbi Kook is respectful of rational thinking, and believes it may have salutary effects on one's spiritual path. Thus, in his essay, "Concerning the Conflict of Opinions and Beliefs," Rabbi Kook notes:

"The world is continually progressing, sound thinking continues to make headway, healthy logic and the rich fund of experience are removing the roadblocks, error is diminishing, the *entanglements of the imagination* are being released." (Bokser, 1978, p. 274, italics added)

In his comment on the "entanglements of the imagination," Rabbi Kook—somewhat surprisingly—does sound a bit like Spinoza, attempting to clear away our "inadequate ideas." Of course, for Rabbi Kook—and perhaps not for Spinoza—our "sound thinking" and "healthy logic" are all in the service of a mystical and spiritual goal; i.e.:

"To find the divine spark hidden in everything, and automatically discard every dross…All the sparks will be joined into the most august torch, and all nations will acquire a clear language to call in the name of the Lord." (Bokser, 1978, p. 275)

Nonetheless, we must also recognize Rabbi Kook's endorsement of logical and rational thinking, regardless of, and apart from, its mystical or spiritual objectives.

Rebbe Menachem Mendel Schneerson (1902-1994)

Known by his followers simply as "The Rebbe," Rabbi Menachem Mendel Schneerson was head of the Lubavitcher movement for forty-four years. The Rebbe is of course squarely within the Jewish mystical tradition. Indeed, according to the summaries of the Rebbe's talks provided by Rabbi Simon Jacobson, the Rebbe emphasized that "to begin to understand G-d… we must learn to go beyond our own mind, our own ego, our own tools of perception." Furthermore, "to look for G-d with our eyes, with our intellect, with our logic, would be like trying to capture the sun's light in our hand" (Jacobson, 1995, p. 214).

And yet, we see in the Rebbe the striking paradox seen in many of Judaism's greatest spiritual leaders. For, like his predecessor, Rabbi Shneur Zalman, Rabbi Schneerson also draws on traditional sources of Jewish "rationalism" (Pies, 2008, pp. 139-46). (It is intriguing that the Rebbe studied mathematics and science at the University of Berlin and the Sorbonne). Also in keeping with the tradition of his Chassidic forebears, the Rebbe was intensely interested in how we cope with pain and suffering, fear and anxiety. To those of us in the mental health profession, some of the Rebbe's advice might well have come from a handbook on cognitive-behavioral therapy. For example:

> "To defeat depression, you must introduce a fresh perspective to your thinking. You must begin to replace troubling, destructive thoughts with positive, constructive ones. Think good and it will be good. This is not foolish optimism; this is recognizing the goodness within even a seemingly bad situation… [Furthermore]…the moment you look fear in the eye, it begins to crumble. Use your intellect to harness your emotions." (Jacobson 141)

Frankly, it would be hard to write a more elegant synopsis of REBT! Similarly, the Rebbe has this to say about anxiety:

> "Half of winning any battle is understanding the enemy, and once you understand the root of your fears, you are well on your way to conquering them. This is not to say that you will be freed of all fear and anxiety. They are a part of life. But they must be seen as a sign that something is out of sync in your life… So when you become aware of fear or anxiety, do not give way to depression; instead, attack and improve the situation." (Jacobson, 1995, p. 140)

Indeed, the Rebbe's view on our power to modulate our emotions is uncannily similar to those of Ellis and other cognitive behavioral therapists. We see this in the Rebbe's discussion of setting limits on mourning, which, in its essential teaching, is quite similar to that of Maimonides (Pies, 1997):

"The sages teach us that it would be barbaric not to mourn at all, but that we should not mourn longer than necessary. A week of mourning is sufficient; otherwise, a person's death becomes a presence unto itself, continuously saddening us and impeding our progress in life. But why should we restrain our natural pain and sadness over a loved one's death? Grief is a feeling, after all, and feelings cannot be controlled, can they? Isn't it wrong to set limits and repress our grief...? True, feelings are feelings, but we can choose whether to experience them in a destructive or productive light." (Jacobson, 1995, p. 121)

Cognitive-behavioral therapists often use a technique called "reframing," in which the patient's mode of seeing a predicament is altered by means of a new cognitive "schema." In this regard, consider the Rebbe's approach to the following case:

"A woman came to the Rebbe for a blessing for her father, who was depressed that he had to spend the High Holidays in a hospital. The Rebbe smiled and said, "Tell your father that he should finish the mission he was sent to the hospital for: to inspire the others there to intensify their spiritual commitments." (Jacobson, 1995, p. 92)

Thus, by redefining the problem—not "hospitalized and depressed" but rather, "hospitalized with a mission!"—the

Rebbe acts in the manner of the cognitive therapist; i.e., "The real-life problem itself has not been changed, but the therapist assists the patient to view it from a different perspective so that it no longer appears insurmountable" (Wilkes, 1994, p. 197).

Similarly, with respect to *physical pain*, the Rebbe tells us:

"No matter how difficult it may be, we must do everything possible to not let our emotions overwhelm us...we shouldn't allow our aberrational thoughts and doubts in response to pain to become the new norm." (Jacobson, 1995, p. 127)

To the therapist's ear, the Rebbe may be cautioning the person with severe pain not to give in to thoughts of suicide, or to allow such despair to become "the new norm." Although, for the Rebbe, surmounting pain ultimately involves exploring "our relationship with God" (Jacobson, 1995, p. 128) his view that *we can exert some control over pain* has clear affinities with the more secular position of Ellis and Harper:

"When you are bothered by real life handicaps, such as physical pain that cannot for the moment be eradicated, you will do well to practice sensory-neglect or distraction...if, for example, you have a headache, you can try to forget about it instead of continually telling yourself: 'My, what a terrible headache this is! How can I stand it if it continues?' Or you can deliberately try to think about something pleasant... or you can participate in some distracting activity." (Ellis & Harper, 1961, p. 119)

For the Rebbe, the person in pain needs "to broaden his perspective," realizing that "pain is an opportunity for growth" and a "test that examines how consumed you are with material comfort as opposed to spiritual growth. [Pain is] a challenge to be met with intense determination" (Jacobson, 1995, pp. 131-32). Of course, this is no easy task. The Rebbe tells us that, "Realigning your perspective on life…cannot be done easily. It takes discipline… [and] the concentrated efforts of study, prayer, and good deeds" (Jacobson, 1995, pp. 129-130).

Nonetheless, for the Rebbe—as for Rabbi Abraham Isaak Kook—we must take responsibility for changing ourselves, hard though it may be, before taking on the infinitely harder task of changing the world. Thus, as we noted earlier, the Rebbe tells us:

"Your first responsibility is to yourself, for you can hardly hope to civilize the world at large if your own life is out of sync. We are all responsible for our own conduct; you cannot blame anyone else for your decisions or actions. You cannot blame your parents or your teachers, your employers or your leaders. Nor can you blame G-d for making life so difficult. No matter how intimidating any obstacle may seem, G-d would not have placed it in your path without also providing you with the abilities to overcome it. Therefore, it is your responsibility to do so." (Jacobson/Schneerson p. 154)

It is hard to imagine Albert Ellis disagreeing with any of these assertions, except perhaps with the direct references to God's intentions and plans. The Rebbe also shares with

Ellis and Harper the concept of what I would call, "beneficial creative engagement." For example, Rabbi Schneerson writes:

> "You can distract yourself [from material concerns]... by focusing on the positive—your achievements, your abilities, the people you love. Better yet, share your anxiety with friends or family members who will give you support, a fresh perspective, and positive suggestions. Get involved in projects that are profoundly gratifying. Soon enough, your life will be so full of meaningful activity that there will be no time for fear and anxiety." (Jacobson, 1995, p. 141)

This advice is very close to that of Ellis and Harper, in their chapter on "Overcoming Inertia and Becoming Creatively Absorbed:"

> "You should make a definite attempt to become vitally absorbed in some persons or things outside yourself. Loving persons rather than things or ideas has some distinct advantages: since other people can, in turn, love you back and can beautifully interact with you. But loving some long-range activity or idea—such as being vitally attached to an art or a profession—also has its great rewards...it is wise to choose a challenging, long-range project or area rather than something simple or short-ranged." (Ellis & Harper, 1961, pp. 180-81)

Finally, there is little doubt that Ellis, Harper, Cohen, and other cognitive therapists would endorse the Rebbe's admonition:

"Instead of wasting our time dwelling on the negative, we should be concentrating on all the good that we can accomplish." (Jacobson, 1995, p. 264)

Rabbi Kalonymus Kalman Shapira (1889 -1943)

The overused term "tragic" hardly begins to capture the anguish and poignancy of Rabbi Kalonymus Kalman Shapira's life—and death. A gifted young rebbe living in Pre-Holocaust Poland, Rabbi Shapira lived through three years in the Warsaw ghetto, only to perish, in 1943, in the death camp at Treblinka (Shapira, 1995). Remarkably, before he was taken to Treblinka, Rabbi Shapira managed to bury a fragmentary diary in the ruins of the Warsaw Ghetto—which work forms the basis for Yehoshua Starrett's translation and commentary.

On one level, discussing Rabbi Shapira in the context of "psychology" is more than a little ironic. Rabbi Shapira evidently held what he termed "today's secular psychologists" in deep contempt. He writes in his journal:

"All these people find in human nature is what they look for because it interests them: vulgar thoughts and filthy fantasies…they themselves are looking at the spiritual dunghill of a decadent humanoid being—the filthy thoughts and indecent desires to which they are also privy." (Shapira, 1995, pp. 152-53)

This is heady stuff indeed! Presumably, Rabbi Shapira was reacting to what he had learned of "Freudian" theories concerning infantile sexuality, repressed desires, etc. In fact, he is clearly aware of the "psychological, ego defense system" invoked in psychoanalytic theory, as well as the role of the unconscious in human life (Shapira, 1995, p. 140). When Rabbi Shapira alludes to the "thick protective shell of selfishness" that "grows around" the self (Shapira, 1995, p. 140), he is clearly invoking the ideas of Freud and his followers—perhaps referring to what one of Freud's disciples, Wilhelm Reich, called "character armor."

But notwithstanding Rabbi Shapira's contempt for psychoanalysis, there are elements of his thought that are strongly in accord with cognitive-behavioral therapy and REBT. For example, Rabbi Shapira endorses the concepts that "each of us is responsible for healing the dysfunction of his own soul" (Shapira, 1995, p. 10), and that this healing occurs through "a long learning process" (Shapira, 1995, p. 11).

It is true that for Rabbi Shapira—in contrast to Ellis, for example—the goal of self-healing requires that one "uproot all untoward desire from [the] soul" (Shapira, 1995, p. 10). And, to be sure, other elements of Rabbi Shapira's philosophy are markedly at odds with REBT, such as when—rather curiously— he admonishes us to "become enraged when negative drives cloud your mind or emotions" (Shapira, 1995, p. 39).

We should not paper over such radical departures from the REBT/CBT paradigm. But despite these differences between Rabbi Shapira and secular cognitive-behavioral therapists, there are also some striking similarities. We may summarize these in the following bullet points that express Rabbi Shapira's philosophy in relation to REBT and CBT:

- Putting remorse and yearning into action
- Swimming against public opinion and being truly one's own person

- Fighting for control over one's emotions
- Becoming "master of one's own life"
- Struggling to improve oneself

Putting Remorse into Action

Rabbi Shapira teaches:

> "Remorse over a spiritual slip is positive only if it is followed and complemented by acts of repentance. Otherwise, it may even have a negative effect...the feeling of remorse and anxiety, if not expressed in the world of action and reinforced through a real act of repentance, will just pass and cease to be. Instead of remorse you will just feel relief...from the pangs of remorse." (Shapira, 1995, p. 17)

Similarly, Rabbi Shapira teaches that we must also put "yearning" into action:

> "Yearning is of value only if you put it into action as a driving force for reaching higher levels. Otherwise, it will tend to create within you a subtle despair... [and] in the end, you will stop yearning." (Shapira, 1995, p. 55)

These teachings are strikingly similar in spirit to Ellis's admonition:

> "Resolving to correct your misdeeds in the future will frequently not suffice, any more than resolving to be a

good pianist will make you one. You can only play the piano, or diet, or correct your past errors in the future by work and practice—by literally forcing yourself to follow a new path. Thus, if you want to be moral, you must literally force yourself to be honest, responsible, and non-injurious to others...long-range self-interest and happiness will be achieved only by your own moral behavior." (Ellis & Harper, 1962, p. 110)

Swimming Against Public Opinion and Being True to One's Own "Unique and Individual Self"

Rabbi Shapira observes:

"As a torrent river surges forth...so does the torrent of public opinion sweep along the individual mind. You may not know it, you may even deny it, but you have been brainwashed by common belief...so stay away from the middle of the river, don't be concerned with what people say...Nor can you remain static in this torrent river just by standing firm in your place—you must actively swim against the flow...there may be a limit to how far you can go, but at least you will not be drawn down with the flow." (Shapira, 1995, pp. 19-20)

Ellis and Harper approach this same ideal by discouraging "dire needs for approval" and encouraging a tough-minded individualism:

"Ask yourself what *you* really want to do in life, rather than what *others* would like you to do; and keep asking yourself, from time to time: "Am I doing this thing or refusing to that because *I* really want it that way? Or am I, once again, unthinkingly trying desperately to please others?...In going after what you really want in life, take risks, commit yourself, don't be afraid of making mistakes." (Ellis and Harper, 1961, p. 89)

Similarly, Rabbi Shapira urges:

"Each and every little one of us has not only the right but the obligation to express his unique and individual self. And to the degree that you are able to live in this world from the very center of your unique self, to that degree will you be able to exercise your individual free will." (Shapira, 1995, p. 27)

Fighting for Control over One's Emotions

The concept of modulating and controlling one's emotions—particularly "negative" emotions, such as anger, fear, and hatred—is absolutely central to CBT and REBT. So, too, for Rabbi Shapira, as we are told in his chapter entitled, "Waging the Holy Inner War:"

"This is how you can judge yourself. If, whenever your passions rise to attack you, you smite them back a double blow, not only do you ignore their demands but you perform a mitzvah as well...But if you humbly surrender to the onslaught of your passions without declaring an all-out war, then you should mourn not only for your falling in battle but also for merely having your passions. Your entire life is just an eternal hell." (Shapira, 1995, p. 22)

We earlier cited a teaching from Rabbi Shapira that is not consonant with REBT; namely, the notion that one should become "enraged" when one experiences strong negative emotions. Clearly, this contradicts that general principle of "self-acceptance" that characterizes Ellis's philosophy. On the other hand, when we examine the *context* of Rabbi Shapira's admonition, we find that his teaching is broadly consistent with REBT's views regarding emotional self-control:

> "You cannot ward off your negative drives unless you also hate them. An intent to just not welcome them is not enough—you must actively despise them. They can destroy your life, both spiritual and physical. So train yourself to become enraged when negative drives cloud your mind or emotions. Only then will you be able to control them." (Shapira, 1995, p. 39)

Indeed, Rabbi Shapira's "prescription" for monitoring one's irrational thoughts (he terms them "psychotic") sounds remarkably like that of CBT/REBT, right down to listening to our own "inner self-talk:"

> "The hard truth is, there is no complete cure that will keep every unsound thought from rising to mind, but at least you can reduce the insanity of these thoughts and keep their appearance to a minimum. The way to do this is through heightened self-awareness. Train yourself to watch every thought that comes to mind: *pay attention*

to all your inner self-talk. Listen to what these inner voices are saying, especially those surrounding your emotional weak points." (Shapira, 1995, p. 93, italics added)

Becoming Master of One's Own Life

Closely linked with controlling one's emotions is the larger, existential goal of *mastering one's life*. Neither Rabbi Shapira nor the cognitive-behavioral therapists are under any illusions in this regard: they are aware that life often deals us unexpected blows, setbacks, and losses that are well beyond our control. In this regard, Ellis and Harper facetiously cite the philosopher Bertrand Russell, who quipped, "Any man who maintains that happiness comes wholly from within should be compelled to spend thirty-six hours in rags, in a blizzard, without food" (Ellis and Harper, 1961, p. 125). And yet, both Rabbi Shapira and therapists like Albert Ellis believe that with sufficient discipline, we can master many important aspects of our lives. Arguably, Rabbi Shapira sets the bar higher even than Ellis, admonishing us:

> "Train yourself to be the master of all aspects of your life, not only regarding permissible pleasure, but regarding your entire inner life. Let not any natural response be triggered in spontaneous fashion, be it action, a refrain from action, speech or even thought. Become the absolute and ultimate master of your inner world so that it reacts not to external influence but only to your deepest command." (Shapira, 1995, p. 49)

To the professional psychotherapist's ear, these exhortations have a rather grandiose ring to them—*nobody* actually succeeds in mastering every "natural response," no matter how rational and self-disciplined the person! However, Rabbi Shapira is speaking in the tradition of many Stoic sages, such as Epictetus (Pies, 2007), who *do* set the bar very high in the matter of self-mastery. And even Ellis and Harper offer a more nuanced variation on Rabbi Shapira's grandiloquence. Thus, in a chapter entitled, "Controlling Your Own Destiny," Ellis and Harper write:

> "The main point…which you must note and believe in this connection is that you are in your own saddle. You can never expect to be deliriously happy at all times in life. Freedom from all physical pain is never likely to be your lot. But an extraordinary lack of mental and emotional woe may be yours—if you think that it may be and work for what you believe in." (Ellis and Harper, 1961, p. 131)

Struggling to Improve Oneself

In a sense, one could argue that all psychotherapeutic and religious schools of thought are engaged in promoting some type of "self-improvement"—there is surely nothing newsworthy in that observation. However, unlike some forms of psychotherapy, in which "self-improvement" is not explicitly set forth as a goal, Ellis's REBT calls for just such a program. For example, in his book *Overcoming Resistance*, Ellis specifically notes the importance of "self-improvement homework" (Ellis, 2007. p. 44). Similarly, in *The Cognitive-Behavioral Workbook for Depression,* Knaus and Ellis write that, "when you work at promoting self-acceptance, you are likely to…stretch for self-improvement" (Ellis & Knaus, 2006, p.169). So, too, the spiritual program set forth by Rabbi Shapira calls explicitly for self-improvement. At the same time—like Ellis—Rabbi Shapira is aware that self-improvement is often a path marked by setbacks, and is different for every individual. Thus, in his chapter on "Personal Rules for Spiritual Growth," Rabbi Shapira observes:

> "Someone who is constantly involved in the inner struggle for self- improvement sometimes wins and sometimes loses. From experience, conclusions can be drawn: when you do this, you win; when you do that, you lose...each person must draw up his own guidelines and self-advice, which will be different from any other's, each tailored for his own unique inner experience." (Shapira, 1995, pp. 123-24)

Ellis and Harper would agree with this "realistic" assessment, but undoubtedly would add that *improving oneself in particular areas* should not be confused with *becoming a better person*—"personhood" being a status Ellis has always seen as distinct from one's *abilities* in some particular area. Thus, Ellis and Harper write:

> "Strive, if you will, to be a better artist, ballplayer, or business man than you now are; but do not delude yourself that you will be a better *person* if you achieve your goal. Strongly desire and work for success in your chosen fields; but be ready to accept failures as undesirable but not dreadful—as having nothing whatsoever to do with your intrinsic value as a human being." (Ellis and Harper, 1961, p. 186)

CHAPTER 8:
CONCLUSION

═══════════

Having surveyed the deep and abiding connections between rabbinical Judaism and cognitively-based psychotherapy, what general conclusions may we draw? And what are the implications of these, for both CBT and Judaism? I believe that a brief reply may be given by focusing on three core issues.

First, it seems to me that pride of place must be accorded one central and foundational principle, common to both rabbinical Judaism and CBT/REBT: namely, the almost supernal importance placed upon *human reason*. Indeed, the term "supernal" (celestial; heavenly) is applicable in a nearly literal sense, in so far as the rabbinical view of man's rational powers is concerned. As the *Encyclopedia of Judaism* (2002) puts it:

> "Many medieval Jewish philosophers held that human reason is a gift from God, so that in principle there could be no conflict between the conclusions of reason and the content of Divine Revelation."

While most cognitive-behavioral therapists do not impute such divinity to human reason, they clearly accord it a place of high honor. Indeed, Elliot Cohen's "Logic-Based Therapy" (LBT) sees the central "mission of psychology" as one of scrutinizing our reasoning "for [the presence of] dangerous premises" (Cohen, 2007, p. 6).

Perhaps the second most important principle common to both rabbinical Judaism and CBT is the conviction that *human beings can exercise their reason in the service of self-improvement, self-control, and self-discipline.* Nowhere is this put more forcefully—and radically—than in the teachings of Maimonides. To cite a previously-quoted passage from his *Guide for the Perplexed* (Part I, chap LXXII):

> "Man has been endowed with intellectual faculties which enable him to think, consider and act...and to *control every organ of his body*, causing both the principal and secondary organs to perform their respective functions." (Maimonides, 1956, p. 118, itaclics added)

Though Ellis and other cognitively-oriented therapists would not go as far as Rambam, they do share his general conviction that we have substantial control over even our biological responses. Thus, in a personal revelation, Ellis discloses:

> "Years ago, I...discovered that I could eliminate most of the pain of drilling or other dental work by deliberately focusing, when my dentist was hacking away at my teeth or gums, on recent pleasant

experiences (especially sexual experiences...or by composing songs in my head while sitting in the dental chair." (Ellis and Harper, 1961, p. 119)

Third, and in some ways, most radically, both CBT and the rabbinical literature endorse the *primacy of behavior* as a means of changing one's mood, attitude, and even *character*. In effect, both traditions argue that—however you may "feel inside"—if you change your behavior, you will begin to change your mood and attitude. Thus, therapist Eliot Cohen notes that

"Aristotle would...remind you that you become the sort of person you are by repeatedly doing the same things. You create your own irrational inclinations by continually acting irrationally...if you repeatedly retreat from social contexts, you will make yourself reclusive, and it will become increasingly more difficult to control yourself....Behavioral therapy takes its cue from Aristotle by realizing that a constructive way to change bad habits is to change your behavior." (Cohen, 2007, p. 125)

Similarly, in his letter to his son, Rabbi Moshe ben Nachman (Ramban) instructs us:

"Get into the habit of always speaking calmly to everyone. This will prevent you from anger... [then]... Once you have distanced yourself from anger, the quality of humility will enter your heart." [*Iggeres HaRamban*]

Commenting on Ramban's instructions for walking and talking in a humble manner, even if one harbors feelings of arrogance, Rabbi Dr. Twerski adds:

"If one adopts these behaviors, it is likely that they will impact on him so that he indeed begins to *feel* humble." (Twerski, 1999, p. 207)

These ideas are radical in the world of psychotherapy, because they completely upend the conventional notion that *one's attitude and emotion determine one's behavior*. Although this is true in many circumstances, both the cognitive-behavioral and rabbinical perspectives argue that *one's behavior often determines one's attitude and emotions*—especially if the behavior is repeated frequently and consistently.

Finally, I believe that our investigation suggests ways in which CBT and REBT may be harmoniously "woven" into the religious individual's world view—and perhaps vice versa. This, indeed, is the focus of the paper by Albert Ellis, cited at the beginning of this book. As Ellis notes:

"Rational emotive behavior therapy (REBT) has been found by many religiously oriented therapists, including Christian, Jewish, and Islamic practitioners, to be quite compatible with religious views…This appears to be particularly true of some of the REBT and benevolent religious philosophies of self control and change; unconditional self-acceptance; high frustration tolerance; unconditional acceptance of others; the desire rather than the dire need for achievement and for approval; the acceptance of responsibility; the acceptance of self-direction; the acceptance of life's dangers; the philosophy of nonperfectionism; and the philosophy of accepting disturbance." (Ellis, 2000, p. 31)

It will be intriguing, in light of Ellis's analysis, to see if REBT can now incorporate various religious and, in particular, *Judaic concepts* into its framework—at least, when REBT is used in the service of observant Jewish patients and clients. For example, Rebbe Menachem Mendel Schneerson describes a "meaningful day" in terms of *gratitude* toward God:

> "When you awake in the morning...think for a moment. What does it mean to be awake and alive? Begin each day with a prayer; thank G-d for the new day. Acknowledge your soul and the vibrancy and fortitude it provides...You discover sanctity and holiness in everything you do. When you eat, you are not just satisfying your hunger...but giving your body and soul the nourishment to help you become a better person. ..Even sleep takes on a new dimension...[it] becomes an opportunity to rejuvenate your soul." (Jacobson, 2005, pp. 146-47)

For the most part, REBT and CBT emphasize the mitigation of unpleasant, "dysphoric" emotions via the elimination of irrational and self-destructive ideas. This is fine as far as it goes—but what about the *affirmation of positive character traits*, such as gratitude for what one has been given; joyful acceptance of life's vicissitudes; and an awareness of how precious even life's small pleasures are? Can these values also be incorporated into the secular, rational framework of REBT and CBT? Arguably, it is not the role of any psychotherapeutic school to inculcate "values"—but this argument is easily overturned by examining the values so vigorously promoted by cognitive therapists; e.g., adherence to rational analysis, the use of "logic," tough-mindedness in the face of adversity, etc. In essence, there is a wide range of Stoic values that are implicit—and sometimes explicit—in the philosophy of CBT (Pies, 2007). If that is the case, there seems no reason why these values cannot be expanded to include some found in Judaism or other faiths. In short, there is reason to envision a *dialectical relationship* between Judaic values and those of cognitive-behavioral therapy, in which each world-view will be enriched and deepened.

END

REFERENCES

Abrams J. Z. *The Talmud for Beginners* (vol. 1). Northvale, NJ: Jason Aronson, 1991.

Albert-Ellis-Friends.net (http.//albert-ellis-friends.net/biography.htm).

Artson, B. A. *The Bedside Torah*. Chicago: Contemporary Books, 2001.

Basser T. Maharal of Prague. Pirke Avos. Brooklyn, NY: Mesorah Publications, 1997.

Beck, A. T. *Cognitive Therapy and the Emotional Disorders*. New York: International Universities Press, 1976.

Beyda R. *Successful Failure.* (2004). Accessed 12/18/09 at http.//www.torah.org/learning/reflections/classes/reflection-59.html

Bokser, B. Z (translator). *The Talmud. Selected Writings.* New York: Paulist Press, 1989

Bokser, B. Z. *Abraham Isaac Kook.* Mahwah, NJ: Paulist Press, 1978.

Bokser, B. Z. *The Jewish Mystical Tradition.* New York: The Pilgrim Press, 1981.

Borchsenius, P. *The History of the Jews.* New York: Simon and Schuster, 1965.

Brown, R., Bottiglieri T., and Colman, C. *Stop Depression Now.* New York: GP Putnam's Sons, 1999.

Bulka, R. P. "Psychological Formulations in the Works of Maimonides." In *Moses Maimonides, Physician, Scientist, and Philosopher,* edited by F. Rosner and S. Kottek . Northvale, NJ: Jason Aronson, 1993:135-143.

Bulka, R. P. *Chapters of the Sages. A Psychological Commentary on Pirkey Avoth.* Northvale, NJ: Jason Aronson, 1993b.

Burtt, E. A. *The Teachings of the Compassionate Buddha.* New York: Penguin Books, 1982.

Cohen, E. D. "Logic-Based Therapy. The New Philosophical Frontier for REBT." REBT Network, 2006. Accessed at. http.//www.rebtnetwork.org/essays/logic.html

Cohen, E. D. *The New Rational Therapy* (Forward and contributions by Albert Ellis). Lanham, MD, Rowman & Littlefield, 2007.

Dan, J. *Jewish Mysticism and Jewish Ethics*. Northvale, NJ: Jason Aronson, 1996.

DeAngelis, T. "Goodbye to a Legend. APA Online." *Monitor on Psychology*, Volume 38, No. 9. October 2007. Accessed 12/18/09 at http://www.apa.org/monitor/oct07/goodbye.html

Ellis, A., and Harper, R. A. *A Guide to Rational Living*. North Hollywood, CA: Wilshire Book Company, 1961.

Ellis, A. "Can Rational Emotive Behavior Therapy (REBT) Be Effectively Used with People Who Have Devout Beliefs in God and religion?" *Professional Psychology Research and Practice*. 2000: 31.29-33.

Ellis, A. Commentary (on Pies). *Voices* (American Academy of Psychotherapists). Winter 2000.

Ellis, A. *Overcoming Resistance*. New York: Springer Publishing, 2007

Epstein, I. *Judaism*. New York: Penguin Books, 1977.

Feldman, Y. Spiritual Excellence. Jewish Classics of the Spirit in Brief. Book One: Bachya Ibn Pakudahh, *The Duties of the Heart*. Project Genesis, 2009.

Feuer, A. C. *A Letter for the Ages. An Exposition on Nachmanides' "Iggeres Ramban."* Brooklyn, NY: ArtScroll/Mesorah Publications Ltd., 1989.

Finkelman, S., and Berkowitz Y. *Chofetz Chaim. A Lesson a Day.* Brooklyn, NY: Mesorah Publications, 1995.

Foxbrunner, R. A. *Habad.* Northvale, NJ: Jason Aronson, 1992.

Friedlander, M. (translator). *The Guide for the Perplexed by Moses Maimonides*, 2nd ed. New York: Dover Publications, 1956.

Frosh, S. "Psychoanalysis, Nazism and 'Jewish science.'" *International Journal of Psycho-Analysis* 84, 2003:1315-1332

Glatzer, N. N. *The Judaic Tradition.* Boston: Beacon Press, 1969.

Goldberg, H., and Salanter, Israel. *Text, Structure, Idea.* New York: Ktav Publishing, 1982.

Green, A. *Tormented Master. A Life of Rabbi Nahman of Bratslav.* New York: Schocken Books, 1981.

Guttmann, J. *The Philosophy of Judaism.* Northvale, NJ: Jason Aronson, 1988.

Halkin, A, and Hartman, D. *Epistles of Maimonides. Crisis and Leadership.* Philadelphia: The Jewish Publication Society, 1985.

Henoch, C. *Ramban. Philosopher and Kabbalist.* Northvale, NJ: Jason Aronson, 1998.

Ibn Chaviv, Y. *Ein Yaakov.* Translated with commentary by A.Y. Finkel. Northvale, NJ: Jason Aaronson, 1999.

ibn Paquda, B., *Duties of the Heart.* Translated by Yaakov Feldman. Northvale, NJ: Jason Aronson, 1996.

Jacobs, L. *Jewish Mystical Testimonies.* New York: Schocken Books, 1977.

Jacobs, L. *Oxford Concise Companion to the Jewish Religion.* Oxford: Oxford University Press, 1999.

Jacobs, L. *The Schocken Book of Jewish Mystical Testimonies.* New York: Schocken Books, 1996.

Jacobson, S. *Toward a Meaningful Life.* New York: William Morrow & Co., 1995.

Katz, M, and Schwartz, G. *Swimming in the Sea of Talmud.* Philadelphia: The Jewish Publication Society, 1997.

Knaus, W.J, and Ellis, A. *The Cognitive Behavioral Workbook for Depression. A Step-by-Step Program.* Oakland, CA: New Harbinger Publications, 2006.

Kranzler, H.N. "Maimonides' Concept of Mental Health and Mental Illness." In *Moses Maimonides, Physician, Scientist, and Philosopher*, F. Rosner and S. Kottek, Eds. Northvale, NJ: Jason Aronson, 1993:49-57.

Kushner, L. *The Way into Jewish Mystical Tradition*. Woodstock, VT: Jewish Lights Publishing, 2001.

Lieber, M., [commentary] *Pirke Avos Treasury*. N. Scherman, Ed. Brooklyn, NY: Mesorah Publications, 1995.

Maimonides, M. *The Guide for the Perplexed*. Translated by M. Friedlander. 2nd ed. New York: Dover Publications, 1956.

McGaugh, JL. "Make Mild Moments Memorable—Add a Little Arousal." *Trends Cogn Sci*. August 2006: 10.345-7

Meier, L. *Jewish Values in Psychotherapy*. Lanham, MD: University Press of America, 1988.

Melber, J. *The Universality of Maimonides*. New York: Jonathan David Publishers, 1968.

Mindel, N. *The Philosophy of Chabad*. Brooklyn: Kehot Publication Society, 1973.

Minkin, J. S. *The Teachings of Maimonides*. Northvale, NJ: Jason Aronson, 1987.

Morinis, A. "Everyday Holiness. The Jewish Spiritual Path of Mussar." Boston, MA, Trumpeter/Shambhala Publications, 2007.

Nachmanides. Iggeres HaRamban. Accessed 10/11/10 at: http://www.pirchei.co.il/specials/ramban/ramban.htm

Nadel, S. M., and Sefer Maggidei HaEmes. [Anthology cited in Stern, 1999—publishing data unobtainable]

Naor, B. "Rav Kook on Homosexuality." 1998. Accessed 10/11/10 at: http.//www.orot.com/hms.html

Next Bible. http.//next.bible.org/lexicon/hebrew/03198

Online Parallel Bible, Young's Literal Translation. Accessed 12/07/09 at: http.//yltbible.com/genesis/21.htm

Orthodox Union. "Great Leaders of Our People: Rabbi Judah Loew, The Maharal of Prague." Accessed 12/08/09 at: http.//www.ou.org/pardes/bios/maharal.htm

Pelkovitz, R. (translation.) and Sforno, O. *Commentary on Pirke Avos.* Brooklyn, NY: Mesorah Publications, 1996.

Pies, R. *Everything Has Two Handles. The Stoic's Guide to the Art of Living.* Lanham, MD: Hamilton Books, 2008.

Pies, R. "Hume's Fork and Psychiatry's Explanations. Determinism and the Dimensions of Freedom." *Psychiatric Times.* Vol. 24, No. 9. August 1, 2007.

Pies, R. Integrating the Rational and the Mystical. the insights and methods of three Hassidic Rebbeim. *Hakirah, the Flatbush Journal of Jewish Law and Thought.* Volume #6, Summer 2008: pp. 139-46.

Pies R: The Judaic foundations of rational-emotive behavioural therapy. *Mental Health, Religion & Culture*, vol. 13, June, 2010, pp. 1-13.

Pies, R. "Maimonides and the Origins of Cognitive-Behavioral Therapy." *Journal of Cognitive Psychotherapy* 1997: 11.21-36.

Pies, R. "Symptoms, Suffering, and Psychodynamics. A Personal Journey from RET to the Talmud Voices." *American Academy of Psychotherapists*, Winter 2000: pp. 61-70.

Proverbs (A. Cohen, translator), *Hindhead*, Surrey: Soncino Press, 1945.

Runes, D. D. *The Ethics of Spinoza*. New York: Citadel Press, 1957.

Savitz, H. A. "Maimonides' Hygiene of the Soul." *Annals of Medical History* 4: 80-86. 1932.

Scruton, R. *Spinoza*. New York: Routledge, 1999.

Seddon, K. *Epictetus' Handbook and the Tablet of Cebes*. London: Routledge, 2005.

Seligman, M. E. P. *Learned Optimism*. New York: Pocket Books, 1990.

Severy, M. (Editor). *Great Religions of the World*. National Geographic Society, 1971

Shapira, K. K. *To Heal the Soul.* Y. Starrett, editor and translator. Northvale, NJ: Jason Aronson, 1995.

Shapiro, D. S. "Wisdom and Knowledge of God in Biblical and Talmudic Thought." *Tradition*. 1971, volume 12 (Fall). Accessed 1/19/09 at.
http://www.lookstein.org/articles/wisdom_knowledge.htm

Sherwin, B. L., and Cohen, S. J. *Creating an Ethical Jewish Life*. Woodstock, NY: Jewish Lights Publishing, 2001.

Spinoza, B. *Ethics (1677)*. Translated from the Latin by R.H.M. Elwes (1883)MTSU Philosophy WebWorks Hypertext Edition © 1997. Accessed 12/13/09 at.
http://frank.mtsu.edu/~rbombard/RB/Spinoza/ethica3.html

Steinberg, D. *On Spinoza*. Belmont, CA: Wadsworth, 2000.

Steinsaltz, A. *Opening the Tanya,* San Francisco: Jossey-Bass, 2003.

Stern Y. *Pirkei Avos With Ideas and Insights of the Sfas Emes and other Chasidic Masters*. Brooklyn, Mesorah Publications, 1999.

Telushkin, J. *Jewish Literacy*. New York: William Morrow, 1991.

Teshima JY. *Zen Buddhism and Hasidism. A Comparative Study.* Lanham. MD: University Press of America, 1995.

The Jewish Publication Society, *Tanakh*, Philadelphia, 1985.

The Oxford Annotated Bible, Revised Standard Version. New York: Oxford University Press, 1962.

Toperoff, S. P. Avot. *A Comprehensive Commentary on the Ethics of the Fathers.* Northvale, NJ: Jason Aronson, 1997.

Twerski, A. J. *Lights Along the Way*, Brooklyn: Mesorah Publications, 1995.

Twerski, A. J. *Visions of the fathers.* Brooklyn: Mesorah Publications, Shaar Press, 1999.

Weiss, R. L., Butterworth, C. *Ethical writings of Maimonides.* New York: Dover Publications, 1975

White, J. R., and Freeman, A. S. (editors). "Cognitive-Behavioral Group Therapy for Specific Problems and Populations." *American Psychological Association*, 2000.

Wilkes, T. C. R., Belsher, G., Rush, A. J., and Frank, E. *Cognitive Therapy for Depressed Adolescents.* New York: The Guilford Press, 1994.

Zelcer, H. "The Jewish Enlightenment" (review essay). *Hakirah*, vol. 6, 2008: pp. 87-118.

ABOUT THE AUTHOR

Ronald Pies, MD, is Professor of Psychiatry and Lecturer on Bioethics & Humanities at SUNY Upstate Medical University, Syracuse, NY. He is also Clinical Professor of Psychiatry at Tufts University School of Medicine and has also been a Lecturer on Psychiatry at Harvard Medical School. He is Editor-in-Chief Emeritus of *Psychiatric Times*. Dr. Pies was graduated from Cornell University and SUNY Upstate Medical Center in Syracuse, NY. He is the author of several textbooks, including *Clinical Manual of Psychiatric Diagnosis and Treatment*, and *Handbook of Essential Psychopharmacology* (both with American Psychiatric Press). He is also the author of a guide to psychotherapy for the general public, *A Consumer's Guide to Choosing the Right Psychotherapist* (Jason Aronson); *Creeping Thyme*, a collection of poems (Brandylane Publishers); a collection of short stories titled *Zimmerman's Tefillin* (PublishAmerica), and *Everything Has Two Handles: The Stoic's Guide to the Art of Living* (Hamilton Books). Dr. Pies's most recent book is *Becoming a Mensch* (Hamilton Books). He lives with his wife, Nancy Butters MSW, near Boston.